CHICAGO'S LAKE SHORE DRIVE
URBAN AMERICA'S MOST BEAUTIFUL ROADWAY

Neal Samors | Bernard Judge

Chicago's Books Press

Edited by Neal Samors, Bernard Judge and
Jennifer Ebeling
Produced by Neal Samors and Bernard Judge
Designed by Sam Silvio, Silvio Design, Inc.
Printed in Canada by Friesens Corporation

For more information on this book
as well as authors' other works visit
www.chicagosbooks.com
Email: NSamors@comcast.net,
Bernard40Judge@gmail.com

Front Cover
Lake Shore Drive and North Michigan
Avenue, Looking North, 2010. (Photograph by
Lawrence Okrent, Okrent Associates)

Back Cover
View from Lake Shore Drive Extension under
construction in planned development of the
old U.S. Steelworks. (Photograph courtesy of
McCaffery Interests)

ISBN: 978-0-9788663-7-2

To Kimbeth Wehrli Judge

To Freddi Samors and
Michael and Jennifer Ebeling

Contents

Early View of Lake Shore Drive, ca 1880s.
(Chicago Historical Society, ICHi-20909,
Photographer-unknown).

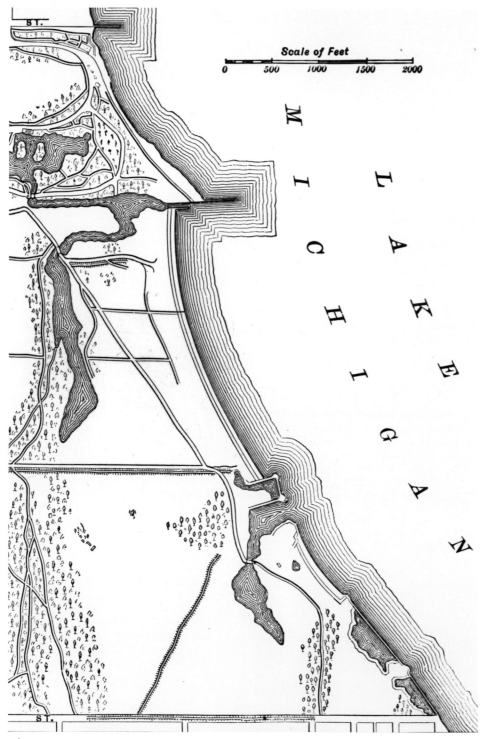

Scale of Feet

0   500   1000   1500   2000

LAKE MICHIGAN

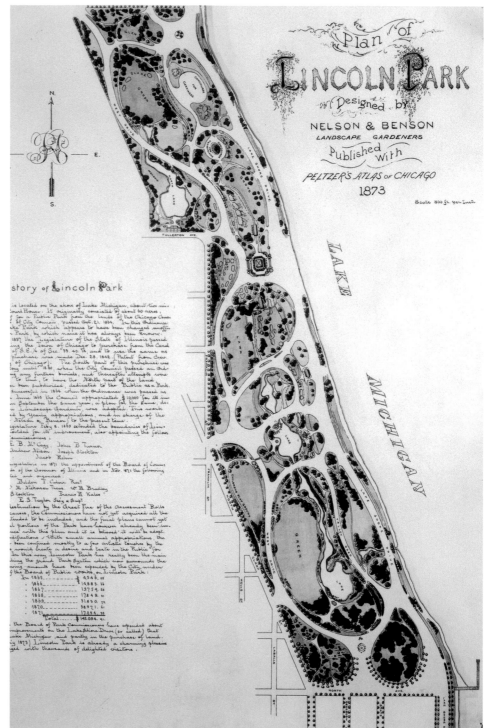

Plan of
LINCOLN PARK
Designed by
NELSON & BENSON
LANDSCAPE GARDENERS
Published with
PELTZER'S ATLAS OF CHICAGO
1873

LAKE MICHIGAN

ACKNOWLEDGMENTS | We want to express our sincerest gratitude to Gary Johnson, President, Chicago History Museum, for writing the wonderful Foreword to the book, his continuous encouragement and support for the creation of this publication, and a willingness to provide the authors with access to the amazing photography collection of the Chicago History Museum. Also, very special thanks are due to Dr. Henry Binford, Associate Professor, Northwestern University, for creating a magnificent Introduction for the book, and thus giving the readers a detailed description of the creation, development and ongoing reshaping of Chicago's Lake Shore Drive.

In addition, a special acknowledgment to Skip Haynes for his essay describing how and why the classic song *Lake Shore Drive* was written and performed and how it became a song enjoyed by countless listeners across America.

The authors offer their deepest appreciation and acknowledgment to the following individuals whose interviews for the book provided us with a wide variety of very personal stories, memories, and opinions about Lake Shore Drive.

Their remembrances and descriptions will give the readers of this book an in-depth understanding of the ways in which a complex "urban road" has connected Chicago from north to south along our beautiful lakefront. Those individuals include: The Honorable Marvin Aspen, Jerome Butler, Blair Camin, Richard Devine, Fr. David Dillon, Philip Enquist, Robert Gordon, the Honorable Neil Hartigan, Daniel McCaffery, JamesMcDonough, the Honorable Abner Mikva, John Norquist, Thomas O'Gorman, Potter Palmer, Warner Saunders, the Honorable Janice Schakowsky, Marc Schulman, Marshall Suloway, Dale Swanberg, Erma Tranter, Daniel Walsh, Richard Ward, and Bill Zwecker.

In addition, special thanks to James McDonough for his financial support of the book project, and to Gary Johnson, Alison Eisendrath, Eric Bronsky, Lawrence Okrent, Robert Allegrini, Daniel Walsh, Dale Swanberg, Daniel McCaffery, Robert Gordon, and Erma Tranter for providing us with access to a wide collection of photographs and maps for use in this publication and for assisting us getting those materials ready for publication.

Jackson Park, September, 1890. In Burnham and Illet, "Book of the Builders, p. 11. (Chicago Historical Society, ICHi-25217).

Plan of Lincoln Park, 1873. (Chicago Historical Society, ICHi-23791, Published with Peltzer's Atlas of Chicago)

I was almost born on Lake Shore Drive. We were on the way from west suburban Forest Park to Wesley Memorial Hospital. My father always told the story the same way: "We had to pull over to the side of the road when we thought you were coming, but then we made a break for it. Thank goodness we were on the only expressway in the city."

Until the network of expressways that we know today was built, our family visits to the city always involved getting to the Drive by any means necessary and staying on the Drive as long as possible. Even for just a mile or two, my father would exult in riding on an expressway.

For someone growing up away from the lake, reaching Lake Shore Drive meant that the world opened up to lakefront views and beaches. This was a boundless horizon that I did not experience except on those rare, exhilarating occasions. I dreamed of living near Lake Michigan, and I am happy to say that my adult life has been spent in Lincoln Park and Evanston, with the water close at hand.

A ride on the Drive also meant being close to people who weren't like us – the rich. We would hear about how my father's Aunt Alma had worked in the Potter Palmer Mansion at 1350 N. Lake Shore Drive back in the days when there were a lot of Swedish maids in town. I can picture "Tant Alma" and her dust mop alone in a room with paintings by Monet and Renoir and Degas, and wonder what went through her head. Now, because of the remarkable generosity of civic leaders such as Bertha Honoré Palmer, I can see those same paintings at the Art Institute of Chicago any day I want – and so can the families of today's immigrant families.

We had a family friend who lived on Marine Drive, one of the north side streets that runs along the Drive. "Aunt Rudi" was a secretary who had an unexplained relationship with her boss that somehow made her quite wealthy. My mother insisted that Rudi had gold plumbing fixtures. Not brass, but gold. I never saw this myself, but I believe my mother, of course. Once a year, my parents would go to a party in Rudi's building, the kind of party where people danced around with lampshades on their heads.

Just the other day, I was in a high rise on Lakeview Avenue. As I faced south over Lincoln Park, I was struck by the delicacy of the fabric of landfills that supports Lake Shore Drive heading north from Oak Street, past beaches, harbors and lagoons.

Lake Shore Drive, of course, is a construct. It was conceived as a feature of the 1909 Plan of Chicago. Through a series of extensions and one remarkable bridge over the Chicago River, the parkway reached Hollywood Avenue to the north in the 1950s. Some still speak of connecting the beaches another couple of miles up Sheridan Road to the Evanston border, but there is no talk any more of extending the Drive that far.

We think of it as one road, but in fact, it was put together in pieces. Southsiders spoke of South Shore Drive, and on the North Side, we spoke of the Outer Drive and the Inner Drive, both as "The Lake Shore Drive." The 'The' seems to have dropped out of parlance thirty years ago, but it still crops up sometimes when I speak today.

The designers did not always get it right the first time. The notorious "S-Curve" was opened by President Franklin Roosevelt in 1937. It included two right-angle turns that brought traffic to a halt until the curve was smoothed out in 1986.

The story of the Drive includes tales from the neighborhoods nearby. Old-timers who remember what it was like before the Drive was built still complain that the highway cut off some of their access to the Lake, but, of course, in those days, the beaches then were nothing like the beaches that we enjoy today – a real string of pearls.

Today, when Friends of the Parks works so zealously to protect the lakeside parks, it is astonishing to learn that the Chicago Park District leased out 88.5 acres of lakefront parkland to the military during the Cold War. Known collectively as "Nike Ajax Missile Base C-84," the missiles were installed in Montrose Harbor, Belmont Harbor, Jackson Park, Burnham Park, Lincoln Park and Rogers Park. The bases were closed in 1963 because the sites could not accommodate the new Nike Hercules missiles. During a quiet moment when you watch the migratory birds at Montrose Point or jog through Burnham Park, think about how much has changed along Lake Shore Drive over the past 50 years.

I remember the sadness surrounding the closing of the Edgewater Beach Hotel in 1967, but its fate was sealed some fifteen years earlier when the extension of Lake Shore Drive from Foster to Hollywood Avenue cut the hotel off from its 1,000 feet of beach frontage. Built in 1916, this grand hotel, which seemed like it belonged in Miami Beach, was a favorite of visiting celebrities. For the generation that came of age during the big band era, broadcasts from the Edgewater Beach Hotel and rare visits to the screened dining room and the outdoor dance floor, were magic. The Edgewater Beach apartment building, built in 1928, is the remaining vestige of that famous complex.

I enjoy a drop-dead gorgeous commute from near the Grosse Point Lighthouse in Evanston to the Chicago History Museum in Lincoln Park. The whole route is Sheridan Road and Lake Shore Drive. I tell people, "It's like Rio, just without the mountains." Don't laugh: a friend from Brazil first told me that.

[1] Gary T. Johnson has been President of the Chicago History Museum since 2005.

Potter Palmer residence, 100 Lake Shore Drive,
ca. 1880s. (Chicago Historical Society,
ICHi-37622, Photographer-unknown).

The Evolution of Lake Shore Drive | To the modern motorist, Chicago's Lake Shore Drive seems to have been laid down in a single grand act of planning. From Jackson Park on the south to Edgewater on the north, it offers a smooth and uniform multi-lane expressway, at once a blessing to commuters, a link between numerous parks and beaches, and a way to dazzle visitors to the city with a continuous spectacle of water and skyline.

But where did it come from? Depending on whom you ask, you may hear that Lake Shore Drive was the work of Daniel Burnham, Potter Palmer, the Park District, or the WPA. All of these answers are, in varying degrees, true. But none of them is adequate to explain the rich and complicated history that produced the Lake Shore Drive of today. The story of this highway is really a set of four overlapping stories. The first three stories begin in the nineteenth century, and concern parallel but at first separate developments on different parts of Chicago's lakefront. One is a story of Lincoln Park, elite land development, and class struggle on the North Side. Another is a story of parks and real estate promotion on the South Side. The third is a story of corporate and municipal relations on the central lakefront near downtown. The fourth story, the one that ties the other three together, is a story of master planning and large-scale government action in the twentieth century.

The origins of Lake Shore Drive lie in popular mid-nineteenth century ideas about re-making urban public space. In many growing cities of the eastern seaboard, worries about congestion, foul air, and the lack of open areas led to proposals for public parks and what were called "scenic drives." The most dramatic of these efforts was New York's Central Park, planned by Frederick Law Olmsted and Calvert Vaux in 1854-55. Their "Greensward" plan included not only a magnificent park, but also a set of carefully conceived paths and carriageways through that park, designed to enable well-heeled city residents to promenade through the beauties of landscaped nature while riding, driving, or strolling among their peers in a fashionable setting. When Central Park was under construction, it became clear that parks and scenic drives were not only pleasant and healthy but also boosted the value of nearby real estate. Residents of other cities took notice of both the attractive and lucrative features of New York's ambitions project

In Chicago, too, there was talk of the need for public parks almost from the beginning of urban development in the 1830s, but meaningful action waited for a few decades. Prosperous Chicago residents who traveled to the East, aware of the big project in New York, wished to follow suit. The full "Olmstedian" vision of large parks with scenic drives blossomed first on Chicago's North Side in the 1860s. The City Cemetery at that time occupied the south end of what is now Lincoln Park. Following a series of lethal cholera epidemics in 1849 and the early 1850s, Dr. John H. Rauch began a crusade against "intramural interments," believing that the burial of disease victims in unstable graves so close to the city posed a public health risk. In response, the city in 1864 banned further burials, and it designated 60 acres of unused land north of the burial ground as a park.

In 1865 it provided for the eventual removal of the bodies from the existing cemetery to more distant burial places, and re-designated the whole area as Lincoln Park, in honor of the recently slain president. A plan for the new park, first drawn by landscape architect Swain Nelson in 1865 and extended north to Diversey Boulevard by Olaf Benson in 1870, included a large lagoon and a variety of roadways, including a drive along the lake front.

Efforts to build such a shore drive, however, were repeatedly undone by storms and wave action. The real birth of Lake Shore Drive came just south of Lincoln Park, through the efforts of Potter Palmer, in the 1880s. Palmer, grown rich through hotel ownership and real estate dealings, had visited Paris, where he was inspired by the extensive re-planning of that city under Napoleon III and Baron Haussmann. In the late 1860s, Palmer led an effort to widen downtown State Street and built a number of grand new buildings that made it into the retail heart of the city. Between 1882 and 1884, he and his wife Bertha built their famous mansion on the lakefront between Oak Street and Lincoln Park, which became a magnet for other wealthy Chicagoans, who built more

homes in the area. Palmer then led his neighbors in a joint project with the Lincoln Park Commission, in which they helped to pay for a seawall and extensive landfill to create a scenic drive as a southern extension of the park past their front doors down to Oak Street. By 1890 this drive had become a tourist attraction, but it was truly just a promenade, ending abruptly on the north in the middle of Lincoln Park, and merging into the narrow and quiet Pine Street on the south.

The extension of Lake Shore Drive east and south from the corner of Oak and Pine was in part a continuation of promotional activity by Palmer and his wealthy neighbors, and in part a response to a challenge they had not foreseen. In 1886, George Wellington Streeter ran his aged steamboat aground in shallow water near Ontario Street. The whole lakefront south of Oak Street to the long seawall protecting the mouth of the Chicago River was an area of accretion through silting. Sand deposited by waves had created dunes, gullies, marshes, and sandbars in a region steadily expanding eastward. Streeter argued that the new land was outside the boundaries of Chicago or Illinois, and therefore open to claim as part of the federal domain. Thus began a decades-long legal, political, and physical struggle between Streeter and the wealthy men who owned the

View of Grant Park during construction with lake and tall ship in distance, ca 1901-1905. (Chicago Historical Society, ICHi-62369, Photographer-unknown).

riparian rights of land east of Pine Street. Streeter was but the most famous of many dubious claimants in this vicinity. The *Tribune* in 1895 ran an article about the area, headlined "Where Squatters and Millionaires Meet."

For landowners who hoped to profit from developing lakefront property, Streeter was a major sand grain in the oyster. Their response was to limit his influence, surround him with higher-end projects, and eventually expel him from the locality. During the 1890s this meant pitched and sometimes fatal battles between police, privately hired guards, and Streeter's squatter supporters. It also meant persuading the city to extend east-west streets, graded at a high level, eastward to the water's edge, and then encouraging contractors to dump their trash between these streets to accelerate the process of filling in the land. It meant helping to pay for a massive new seawall and an extension of Lake Shore Drive from the corner of Oak and Pine east and then south around the landfill region down to Ohio Street. Although Streeter continued court battles into the twentieth century, by 1900 he and his followers had been evicted, with only his name left as a label for the region. Meanwhile, the Lincoln Park Commissioners had built more on the northern end, so that by 1910, Lake Shore Drive extended from Ohio Street through Lincoln park to Belmont Avenue.

Meanwhile, a second group of land promoters on the South Side had generated interest in "scenic drives" of a slightly different sort. Paul Cornell was the central figure in this effort. Beginning in the 1850s, he invested money, time, and energy in developing Hyde Park and other nearby areas. He had persuaded the Illinois Central Railroad to open a depot at 57th Street, and was very interested in opening other connections between downtown and his then remote communities to the south. Inspired as well by Central Park and by the beginnings of Lincoln Park, in 1866 Cornell organized a group including Dr. John Rauch to press for more parks, indeed for a whole system of parks for Chicago. He wanted a single overall park commission like the one in New York, but voters rejected this idea. Through conversations with Olmsted himself, Cornell's group then came up with the idea of constructing several big parks surrounding the city and connected by boulevards. This proposal led the state to create three park commissions in 1869, one for each sector—North, West, and South— of the city.

Between 1866 and 1870, Olmsted and Vaux did initial planning for parts of this system, including the two great parks of the South Side, Washington and Jackson. Jens Jensen and Horace Cleveland continued this work after 1872.

Rowhouses along Michigan Avenue overlooking lake, breakwater and factories looking north from Harrison Street, ca 1865. (Chicago Historical Society, ICHi-62330, Photographer-unknown).

Responding to Cornell's lobbying, the city also created wide and landscaped boulevards—Drexel and South Park—linking the South Parks system to downtown. Washington Park, with its extensive interior drives, was essentially finished by the 1880s. Jackson Park was largely undeveloped until the World's Fair of 1893, but Olmsted's work for that Fair, plus Cornell's promotional activities within Hyde Park, produced a stretch of lakefront drive from about 55th Street south through the park by 1900.

By the early twentieth century, therefore, two public-private initiatives had created relatively short and self-contained scenic shore drives near upper-income communities north and south of the city. But in the long stretch of lakefront between these two, the development story was longer and quite different. In 1836, long before Potter Palmer or Paul Cornell had conceived of their projects, the commissioners of the Illinois & Michigan Canal had produced a plat of central Chicago. On the lakefront property east of Michigan Avenue, from Randolph south to 12th Street, they wrote "Public Ground—Common to Remain Forever Open, Clear and Free of Any Buildings, or Other Obstruction Whatever." Since the waterline was at this point only a short distance east of Michigan Avenue, this "public ground" amounted to a narrow strip of land.

It nevertheless made Michigan Avenue into a sort of lakefront promenade in the years just before the Civil War.

Water erosion, however, was a constant problem. In 1851 the Illinois Central Railroad, seeking access to the downtown area, proposed to build a seawall protecting the central lakefront in return for the right to build a viaduct a few hundred feet offshore, bringing its tracks to a station at Randolph Street. The city agreed, and the viaduct went up, creating a stagnant lagoon between rail tracks and shore that rapidly become trashy and odorous. After the Fire of 1871, the city filled the lagoon with debris. But the "public ground" was not maintained, and by the 1880s it had become an eyesore. In 1890, Aaron Montgomery Ward, dismayed by the neglected state of the lakefront and by various commercial and industrial encroachments, began a series of lawsuits based on the Canal Commissioners' 1836 "forever open" notation. Ward's persistence and his deep pockets finally emerged victorious in 1911. In the meantime, his efforts pushed the city to clean up the central lakefront and eventually to transfer its oversight to the South ParkCommission. In 1901 the Commission renamed the area Grant Park, honoring the Union General and President, and in 1907 it hired Olmsted's sons to produce a

Terrace Row, from Breakwater, at Michigan Avenue at Van Buren and Congress, ca 1865. (Chicago Historical Society, ICHi-62327, Photographer-unknown).

formal plan—which included scenic drives. Thus, by 1907, there were extant pieces of a shore drive on the North and South Sides, and a plan for a drive in the center.

The idea of connecting the scenic drives near the lake was bruited about in the 1890s, thus beginning the fourth and final story, the one that joined the pieces. Early ideas, including one proposed by Daniel Burnham in 1896, involved a north-south connection via a widened Pine Street crossing the Chicago River by bridge or tunnel to Michigan Avenue. Burnham's sweeping 1909 Plan of Chicago embodied this idea, but also imagined a continuous drive along the lake with a bridge across the river near its mouth. Burnham always believed that the project would be a series of scenic drives, but when it was actually implemented, the needs of the automobile turned it into something quite different.

Business and city council leaders, inspired by the boldness of Burnham's vision, took up the idea of a connected shore drive in the 1920s. Planners of that decade proposed that the double-decked Wacker Drive should be extended eastward along the river to connect with Lake Shore Drive, and that the new bridge at the river's mouth would have two levels, like the one that was opened in 1920 on Michigan Avenue. The shore drive in Grant Park would be carried directly north to connect with the extension of Wacker Drive. (This plan was the reason

for the notorious 90-degree turns that bedeviled drivers between South Lake Shore Drive and the bridge from 1937 until 1986, when the southern approach to the bridge was relocated and the turns were smoothed out.) Planning for the approach ramps to what was called the Link Bridge began in 1926, but the Depression postponed completion of the bridge itself. Meanwhile, the South Park Commission gained riparian rights to all of the shore between Grant Park and Hyde Park in 1919, and a rapid process of landfill expanded the shoreline from 14th to 57th by 1930. Extension of Lake Shore Drive southward followed quickly behind the fill process, reaching 57th by 1932. On the North Side, the Park Commission managed to extend the drive to Foster Avenue before state aid ran out in 1932. The extension from Belmont to Foster was a multi-lane divided highway, and it included the first series of multiple cloverleaf interchanges in the United States.

In the early years of the Great Depression, construction of the shore drive halted, but landfill and construction for the Century of Progress Exhibition of 1933-34 kept public attention focused on the central lakefront. When federal aid for public works became available in 1933, Chicago was an early beneficiary because of its existing plans and its strong Democratic Party

Lake Shore Drive with sea wall on right and houses on left, 1890. (Chicago Historical Society, ICHi-35726, Photographer-J.W. Taylor).

Henry Graves residence, Lake Shore near 33rd Street, post 1871. (Chicago Historical Society, ICH1-23946, Photographer-unknown).

S.E. Gross Residence, Division Street and Lake Shore Drive, ca 1880s. (Chicago Historical Society, ICHi-14144, Photographer-unknown).

Michigan Avenue, south of Jackson, 1889. (Chicago Historical Society, ICHi-21987, Photographer-unknown).

connections. The Link Bridge was finished and dedicated by President Roosevelt in 1937, thus completing a multi-lane highway from Jackson Park north to Ohio Street. Additional federal funds allowed the expansion of the old four-lane drive from Ohio up to Belmont by 1942, where it joined the wider extension already built. By 1942, Chicago had its modern multi-lane automobile highway from 57th Street to Foster Avenue.

The remaining changes to produce the Drive of today came after World War II. In 1955 the Park District extended Lake Shore Drive north to Hollywood. On the South Side, the 1950s and 1960s saw a series of large-scale projects that, while not compromising the highway, drastically changed its surroundings. All were surrounded by intense controversy. Beginning in 1957, the building, rebuilding, and expansion of the McCormick Place exhibition center violated the "forever open" principle cherished by Ward and Burnham. In 1964-66 a massive interchange was built to link the drive to the Stevenson Expressway. A plan to widen the Drive through Jackson Park to 67th Street encountered powerful opposition because of the necessary cutting of trees. Five hundred trees were felled, but growing protests prompted the city and the park district to halt the project and produce a scaled-back expansion instead.

Far from being the product of a single unified master plan, Lake Shore Drive was thus a work of many hands, many eras, and many intentions. As we cruise its length today, we can see, here and there, reminders of its various earlier incarnations. On the North Side, the "inner" and "outer" drives remind us of the way the older promenade boulevards were supplanted by massive additional landfill and re-engineering. The dramatic curve at Oak Street, lined by the Drake Hotel and a variety of luxury apartments and condominiums, bear testimony to the power and wealth of those late-nineteenth century investors who went to such lengths to transform sandy lakefront wastes into profitable building sites, and to squeeze out Streeter and his squatting neighbors. Passing the Art Deco towers of the massive Link bridge, and sweeping along the magnificent central lakefront, we can pay homage to the persistence of Aaron Montgomery Ward and the brilliance of Burnham and the other grand planners of the early twentieth century. On the far South Side, the gentle curves of the shore drive through Jackson Park attest to the ambitions of Paul Cornell and the triumph of Olmsted's design for the World's Fair grounds in Jackson Park. With a little imagination, Lake Shore Drive can provide not merely a way to get from one place to another, or to enjoy the lakefront, it can offer a window on the city's complex and intriguing past.

Additional Reading

Carl W. Condit, *Chicago 1910-29: Building, Planning, and Urban Technology.*
(Chicago: University of Chicago Press, 1973

Carl W. Condit, *Chicago 1930-70: Building, Planning, and Urban Technology.*
(Chicago; University of Chicago Press, 1974.)

Harold M. Mayer and Richard C. Wade, *Chicago: Growth of a Metropolis.*
(Chicago: University of Chicago Press, 1969)

Carl S. Smith, *The Plan of Chicago: Daniel Burnham and the Remaking of the
American City.* (Chicago: University of Chicago Press, 2006).

John W. Stamper, *Chicago's North Michigan Avenue: Planning and
Development, 1900-1930* (Chicago: University of Chicago Press, 1991).

Lois Wille, *Forever Open, Clear, and Free: The Struggle for Chicago's Lakefront,*
2nd ed. (Chicago: University of Chicago Press, 1991)

Sheridan Road, south of Grace Street (early 1900's),
reproduction of postcard. (Chicago Historical Society,
ICHi-34690, Photographer-unknown).

Birdseye view of South Michigan Avenue from Adams to Madison Street, showing Grant Park and lakefront railroad, ca 1880. (Chicago Historical Society, ICHi-62349, Photographer-unknown).

9680

JWT

Winding its magnificent way for almost 17 miles along the city's eastern border, Lake Shore Drive is Chicago's beautiful barrier protecting Lake Michigan from defacement and development. No major metropolitan center in the U.S.A. has a comparable roadway.

The story of Lake Shore Drive is the story of Chicago. On the North Side, it came into being through the early 20th century efforts of leaders, such as Potter Palmer, businessman, hotel builder and visionary. Decade after decade its north concrete tentacle crept slowly, ending today at Sheridan Road and Hollywood Avenue.

On the South Side, it was carved out, piece by piece, near the original rail line path that led to the 1893 Columbian Exposition, which was built on what had been a sandy swamp and is now Jackson Park. That World's Fair, the brainchild of architect and planning genius, Daniel Burnham, made it clear that Chicago was ready for the world stage.

In time, the south portion of the Drive paved its way close to where the steel mills and other heavy industries muscled onto the lakefront, providing work for a constant flow of immigrants seeking comfort in Carl Sandburg's "City of the Big Shoulders."

During my formative years, the Drive simply was a daydream route to the rest of America. All I needed was a warm day and a shady tree near the beach along South Shore Drive, which is what the Drive was called in my neighborhood of the same name.

The Drive was also U.S. Highway 41 and if you were in a car driving to or going away from Chicago, you probably used that road. This period of time—from the late '40s to the late '50s—preceded expressways, turnpikes and bypasses.

I'd lean against that shady tree and look at the license plates of passing cars, an endless stream in summer vacation months. Only the very-well-to-do took winter vacations back then.

Mostly I saw plates from Illinois, Wisconsin, Indiana and Michigan. The farther away the state, the less frequently that plate would appear and seeing one was a memorable treat. A California plate promised the Pacific Ocean and exotic Hollywood. New York spoke of the Empire State Building and Broadway. Montana said cowboys and bison and bears. Mississippi sang Ole Man River and the Gulf and Mark Twain characters with slow-talking drawls. Countless little boy summer hours lazily melted away in license plate daydreams.

In the mid-1950s my license plate dreams were replaced with the exciting reality of a driver's license and the freedom to roam that it promised. But driving the Drive was not for beginners. So formidable was it back then with its six ribbons of concrete and asphalt loaded with speeding cars zigging and zagging in heavy traffic, that new drivers stayed off until confidence and skill equaled the challenge of the city's only limited access roadway.

Today the far south end of the Drive remains an everyday street as it cuts through clusters of apartment buildings, houses and commercial structures from beyond 83rd Street to 67th Street where Jackson Park begins and the par-three golf course of the South Shore Cultural Center ends.

In the early twentieth century the Center was an exclusive country club belonging to the likes of the Armours and the Swifts. Later it became a club mostly for moneyed Catholics who couldn't gain admittance to the Protestant-dominated clubs of the rich and famous. The Catholics, learning from example, then excluded Jews from South Shore Country Club membership.

The neighborhood west of the Club changed in the late 1960s from white to African American and the stately club eventually closed. It remained shuttered until the Chicago Park District bought and remodeled it before reopening it for everyone. President Barack Obama held his wedding reception there. A new chapter of Chicago history began.

Originally, Chicago Park District police patrolled the Drive, keeping the road safe and pockets filled for some honesty-challenged enforcers of the law. Lots of breakfasts, lunches and dinners were bought for those hungry men in Park District blue, each of them playing their appropriate role in the human drama of the "City on the Make." The Park District force was absorbed into the regular Chicago Police Department in 1957 and another greasy chapter of city history more or less closed.

Everyone has their favorite spot along the Drive where the city's beauty bursts forth in breathtaking fashion. Some like the view of the Drake Hotel, Oak Street beach, Lincoln Park and the Navy Pier ferris wheel as the Drive travels south of North Avenue beach cruising next to the concrete and steel high rise cliffs on the Drive's western edge.

Others prefer the downtown visual explosion that occurs after the northbound Drive passes under McCormick Place and becomes the instant pathway to a stunning vista of tall and powerful buildings on one side contrasted by the parkland greenery and sparkling waters of Lake Michigan on the other. And right in the middle is Soldier Field and its nesting space ship stadium. More Chicago history made and in the making.

My personal favorite is the northbound side at about 50th Street where the parkland trees part providing a view of the unadorned beauty of the lake's ever-changing colors, and crowned by the city's commercial jewels jutting skyward along the lake's horizon.

Next consider where the Drive and Chicago River intersect. Until the mid-eighties, the Drive there made two maddening 90 degree turns in less than two blocks as it traveled over an ugly tangle of railroad tracks, box cars, warehouses,

German Building in Jackson Park showing carriages and pedestrians, 1900. (Chicago Historical Society, ICHi-62344, Photographer-unknown).

cinder and mud parking lots and other assorted eyesores. Today, in a relatively straight line it traverses boat slips, handsome high rise buildings in Lake Shore East and Streeterville, and acres of new parkland with world famous Millennium Park and Navy Pier only a few blocks away.

The question has to be asked: What other roadway can you take in a matter of minutes to five world class museums, more than a dozen sandy beaches, an immense exhibition hall, a major sports stadium, and a renowned zoo while treating your eyes to the beauty of the azure lake?

The last chapters about the Drive as protector of the lakefront are waiting to be written. Urban planners call it the "final four miles"—the two-mile stretches beyond the north and south ends of the Drive that are now cluttered with apartments, condominiums and commercial structures blocking views of the lake and much of the public from enjoying that lake.

Daniel Burnham's plan for the lakefront to be "forever open and free" is not complete. There are plans for the "final four" on the drawing boards and developers in the wings, such as Daniel McCaffery, waiting to make that happen. All it will take is the money to build and the progressive drive of today's civic leaders who know how to make things happen in the "City that Works."

Lake Shore Drive and Elm Street, 1910. (Chicago Historical Society, ICHi26051, Photographer-Chicago Daily News, DN-008159).

Chicago Harbor, from the Kimball Building, 1891. (Chicago Historical Society, ICHi-03152, Photographer–unknown).

Growing up in Rogers Park on Chicago's Far North Side, my main connection to Lake Shore Drive was Sheridan Road that wound through the eastern edge of the neighborhood and connected with the Drive, at that time, at Foster Avenue. I was born in July, 1943 and it wasn't until the mid-1950s that Lake Shore Drive was extended east of the famous Edgewater Beach Hotel to Hollywood Street.

As far as I was concerned, the extension made driving and riding easier for me because traffic used to crawl along Sheridan to Foster when my family would drive from Rogers Park on the city's north end to my grandparents' apartment in South Shore located south of the Drive and Jackson Park.

Sheridan Road was also an important street in my life because the parks and beaches where I would spend my summers were located along and east of that road, including Touhy Beach, with its tiny field house where basketball shots would usually bounce off the ceiling. In front of that building was a gravel field that served as a baseball diamond in the summer and an ice skating rink in the winter. The legendary Sam Leone ran Touhy Beach as well as having overall responsibility for training and managing the lifeguards who were assigned to positions up and down the lakefront from Howard to Hollywood. Just south of Touhy Beach was Loyola Park, its field house, baseball diamonds, handball courts, and beach. Then there were Greenleaf, Lunt and Farwell Beaches.

As a young boy, I remember the magnificent experience of riding on the Drive going south to downtown, manipulating the "S" curve, hoping the bridge there wouldn't be in an elevated position, and then proceeding to South Shore (with a regular stop in Chinatown for lunch). But, the best part of the trip was returning home and proceeding north on the Drive at night with the city all lit up along the glistening lake in summer time and frozen tundra in the winter. In fact, all my seasonal memories still come back when I remember driving on Lake Shore Drive.

When I was growing up, Lake Shore Drive was the direct roadway connection between my neighborhood and such places as Lincoln Park, Wrigley Field, downtown Chicago, the Field, Shedd and Adler museums, Grant Park, Soldier Field and the Museum of Science and Industry. When I learned to drive in 1960, the final test assigned to me by my driving school instructor was to enter the Drive at Hollywood and go south to Lawrence, just to have some brief time surviving as a young driver on a busy expressway.

By the time I was able to drive my father's car, or when I owned my first car, Lake Shore Drive was a wonderful way to view the city from its many perspectives. There was the beauty of entering the Magnificent Mile at Oak Street to either see a movie at the Esquire Theater, drive down Boul Mich past stores that were beyond my price range, or crossing the Michigan Avenue Bridge and exploring downtown.

If I drove as far south as Hyde Park, the University of Chicago, and the Museum of Science and Industry, that meant I was in another world with its own distinct features and neighborhoods. When I would return from college for breaks

or during the summer, I would look forward to getting on the Drive because it reinforced my strong sense of "being home" and back in Chicago. That feeling about the Drive has never changed.

As the years have gone on, my emotional reaction to being on the Drive is one of awe and appreciation. I have traveled around the country and visited all of our great American cities and I never seen or driven on a roadway that compares with Lake Shore Drive with the beautiful lake, magnificent parks, breathtaking downtown skyscrapers, and changing neighborhoods that abut the Drive from north to south. The most amazing thing to me has always been the fact that the city's political, business and spiritual leaders have worked closely together to keep the lakefront free of industry and any type of artificial barrier that would destroy the view of the city and the lakefront.

Gambling house located on Sheridan Road, viewed from across the street, with automobile parked in driveway, 1927. (Chicago Historical Society, DN-0083896, Photographer–Chicago Daily News).

View north on Lake Shore Drive from Goethe Street, ca. 1920. (Chicago Historical Society, ICHi-26033, Photographer-unknown).

Edgewater Beach Hotel, ca 1920. (Chicago Historical Society, ICHi-16101, Photographer–unknown).

CHAPTER 1
CHICAGO'S LAKEFRONT IN THE EARLY YEARS 1833–1909

1833
Village of Chicago established.

1833
One thousand foot pier built from
north side of the Chicago River that created
harbor south of the mouth of the river.

1835
On November 2, citizens of Chicago gathered
at a meeting and decided that half of the former
Fort Dearborn, bounded by Michigan Avenue,
Chicago River, Lake Michigan and Madison
Street belonged to the town and was to be
used "for all time to come, for a public square,
accessible at all times to the people."

1836
Gurdon Hubbard, William F. Thornton and
William B. Archer platted canal lands that
would become part of the Illinois & Michigan
Canal. The plat identified property east of
Michigan Avenue, from Madison Street south
to 12th Street (Roosevelt Road) as "Public

Ground—Common to Remain Forever
Open, Clear and Free of Any Buildings, or Other
Obstruction Whatever."

1839
Exact boundaries of Ft. Dearborn land were
determined in April by Federal Government
when the rest of the Fort Dearborn tract went
on sale.

1851
Illinois Central Railroad offers to construct
seawall east of Michigan Avenue, south of the
Chicago River. Chicago gives railroad a 300
foot strip 400 feet east of the west side of
Michigan Avenue.

1852
Illinois Central Railroad begins immediately
to construct breakwater from Randolph to 22nd
Street and on a trestle that would shut the south
side of Chicago off from its lakefront. Railroad
acquires slightly less than two acres of old Fort
Sheridan lakefront from Federal Government

north of Randolph to mouth of Chicago River
and fills in lake about 1000 feet east to create a
big tract for passenger terminal and train sheds.

1860
City decides to make a 60-acre cemetery north
of the downtown into a public park because
of concerns that the city's water supply is being
contaminated by the buried bodies. After 1865
Assassination of President Abraham Lincoln,
park is named in honor of him. Bodies were
moved over time from cemetery to others
located further north of the city.

1865
Potter Palmer sells new store on State Street
to Marshall Field and Levi Leiter. Store later
becomes Marshall Fields.

1869
Illinois Legislature passes legislation in which
it agrees to sell a portion of bottom of Lake
Michigan along city's shore to Illinois Central
Railroad. Illinois governor vetoes bill, but

legislature passes it again. The issue was not
finally resolved until U.S. Supreme Court decision
in 1910 when court ruled that the legislature
could repeal the sale of the harbor to the I.C.
and that the lakefront park and harbor belonged
to the city of Chicago.

1869
Lincoln Park Commission is established as a
special district, one of three Chicago-area
park districts. It is given authority over lakefront
land between North and Diversey Avenues.

1870
Bertha Honore marries Potter Palmer in late
July at parents' home at 157 Michigan Avenue
across street from today's site of Art Institute
of Chicago.

1870
Frederick Law Olmsted and Calvert Vaux,
noted landscape designers, are hired by the
South Park Commission to design Jackson and
Washington Parks on city's South Side.

Lakefront at Jackson Park, about 1900.
(Chicago Historical Society, ICHi-29470,
Photographer – unknown).

RICHARD WARD | When they laid out the original plat of Chicago in 1836, three Canal Commissioners were appointed by the governor and approved by the Illinois State Legislature, to sell parcels of land covering 500 square miles. They wanted to build an Illinois-Michigan Canal to connect Lake Michigan with the Illinois water way system that went into the Mississippi River to effectively connect the Atlantic Ocean with the Gulf of Mexico. It was a missing piece of about seven miles long that was called Mud Lake back then and it was a historic, muddy portage area. The only way you could get across that lake (essentially it is where the Stevenson Expressway is now located) was to build the canal. Neither the State of Illinois nor the Federal Government had the money, so they decided that the Federal Government give land to the State of Illinois. They appointed the Canal Commissioners to sell this land to raise money so that they could dig this canal. But they saw an extra value in the land that was right along the lakefront, and they wrote on the original plat of Chicago the famous saying, "Public Ground – A Common to Remain Forever Open, Clear and Free of any Buildings, or Other Obstructions whatsoever." In 1839, the Ft. Dearborn land was being disposed, and they looked at what had been done south of Madison Street and they attempted to mimic the same kind of dedication restrictions that were imposed on the stretch along the lake front. Essentially all they said was "no buildings between the middle of Madison Street (extended east) and the south side of Randolph Street along the lakefront." So, subsequent Illinois Supreme Court decisions combine those two and, effectively, there is a protection all the way between 11th Street and Randolph. The reason it didn't go north of Randolph is because building had already taken place in a three-acre piece of land on the east side of Michigan Avenue between Randolph and the Chicago River. So, the 1839 covenant is between the south side of Randolph and the middle of Madison Street.

In 1833, the city wanted a protected harbor. The waters of Lake Michigan go in a counter clockwise motion coming down the west side of the lake and going up the east side. The city needed a protected pier going out into the lake, and they built one from the north bank of the Chicago River out into the lake some 1000 feet. It went out to where the water cannon is now located. They felt that they could have a protected harbor for the ships waiting to get into the Chicago River to unload and load their goods. So, they built that in 1833. However, what they didn't realize is that they would be making the situation worse for the erosion that would take place during the storm seasons. What they did was, in effect, make a quiet area very near, but, beyond that point it would erode along Michigan Avenue.

World Columbian Exposition, Agricultural Building, 1893. (Chicago Historical Society, ICHi-23347).

So, all the nice homes that were built along Michigan Avenue were more threatened after 1833 because of what they had done here. They didn't put the two ideas together. They had a big problem because all the big money and all the nice homes had the water lapping away near them on Michigan Avenue from Randolph to 11th Avenue.

In about mid-1845 to 1850, they had a debate and went to the Federal Government to try to get money to build a breakwater, but the U.S. Government didn't have any money. Next, they went to the State of Illinois, but since the state was newly admitted in 1818, it didn't have any money. However, the railroads were watching this and they stepped up and said that they would build a breakwater for protection. At the end of the 1840s, the Illinois Central Railroad agreed to build a breakwater, but they wanted to build a trestle on the breakwater. For about two years, the City of Chicago debated the railroad's offer and realized that they didn't have any options. So, they finally agreed, even though they didn't particularly want the railroad out there, but they needed the protection. In about 1850, they allowed the railroad to build the breakwater and the trestle. They started down about 24th Street, and, in a very short time they had the railroad trestle built and then they filled in the land under the trestle to create a breakwater. So, there was protected water between Michigan Avenue and the trestle that was out some 400 feet from the avenue.

Horse-drawn wagon, carriage, and sleigh in street on Michigan Avenue at Grant Park, ca. 1890. (Chicago Historical Society, ICHi- 62328, Photographer-unknown).

South façade of Fine Arts Building at World's Columbian Exposition, 1893. (Chicago Historical Jackson Park Pavilion Shelter, 57th Street and Lake in Jackson Park, About 1900. (Chicago Historical Society, ICHi-16983, Photographer- unknown).

Jackson Park Pavilion Shelter, 57th Street
and Lake in Jackson Park, about 1900.
(Chicago Historical Society, ICHi-16983,
Photographer – unknown).

General Plan of Jackson Park, ca 1900
(Map # 2823). (Chicago Historical Society,
ICHi-27758).

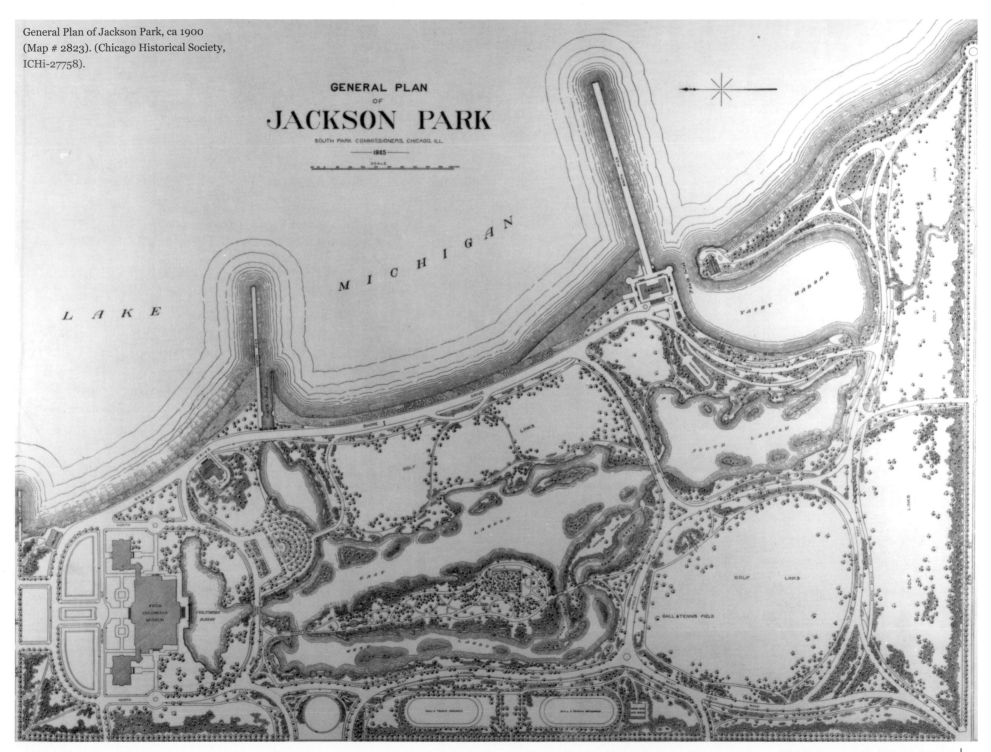

GENERAL PLAN
OF
JACKSON PARK
SOUTH PARK COMMISSIONERS, CHICAGO, ILL.
1895
SCALE

1871
Great Chicago Fire on October 8 destroys much of Chicago from near South Side northward to Fullerton and including Lincoln Park, downtown and Gold Coast.

1872
The lake downtown between Michigan Avenue and the railroad breakwater filled in with debris from the fire. Additional fill added beginning in 1901 when dredging from river harbor and Chicago Drainage Canal.

1872
Potter Palmer builds second Palmer House on State Street which replaces one destroyed by Great Chicago Fire.

1873
Inter-State Exposition Building constructed as center for music, art, commerce and industry on east side of Michigan Avenue.

1874
Frederick Law Olmsted's plan for Washington Park is largely realized, but few improvements were made to Jackson Park until its selection as the location of the 1893 World's Columbian Exposition.

1875
Potter Palmer works with Lincoln Park Board of Commissions to build Lake Drive. It is some 200 feet wide and of a mile long running in front of Potter Palmer house on filled in Frog Pond. Name later changed to Lake Shore Drive as northern extension of Pine Street. In 20th Century, Pine Street becomes North Michigan Avenue.

1881
Jackson Park officially named in honor of President Andrew Jackson, seventh President of the United States.

1882
Potter Palmer begins construction of house designed by Henry Ives Cobb and Charles Sumner Frost which boasts an 80' tower and is served by 27 maids, butlers and social secretaries. House is located at 1350 North Lake Shore Drive and runs for the entire block from Banks to Schiller on land once owned by John Jacob Astor in neighborhood named the Gold Coast. It is referred to as Palmer Castle. The Drive there is a quiet boulevard used for carriage rides along the lakefront.

1885
Palmer Castle is completed, making it the third residence on Lake Shore Drive before Palmer friends from Prairie Avenue begin moving north across river to build their houses in the newly named Gold Coast.

1886
George Wellington "Cap" Streeter and his wife, Maria, run their steamship, Reutan, aground in Lake Michigan about 450 feet from the city's shore. Streeter finds excavation contractors willing to dump fill on the beach near his boat where he eventually amasses 186 acres of newly created land. Based on an 1821 government survey, Streeter determines that his man-made land lies beyond the boundaries of Chicago and Illinois and claims that he is homesteading the land as a Civil War veteran.

1889
Streeter forcibly is removed from his home by Chicago Police on May 4, 1889, but soon returns and hostilities escalate between police and denizens of Streeter's "District."

1890
Aaron Montgomery Ward begins a series of legal battles to reclaim city's lakefront park for open space and public use.

1892
In spite of protests from citizens of Chicago, the U.S. Supreme Court rules that Lake Michigan and its submerged bottom are held in public trust by the state for the people and cannot be sold to a private party.

1892
Inter-State Exposition Building on east side of Michigan Avenue is razed to make way for new building that hosts the World Congresses during the Columbian Exposition of 1893. At the close of the Fair, building becomes the Art Institute of Chicago.

1893
World Columbian Exposition is held in Jackson Park and on the Midway Plaisance in neighborhoods of South Shore, Hyde Park and Woodlawn Frederick Law Olmsted and Daniel Burnham worked together to lay out the grounds for the world's fair. Director of the Exposition is Charles H. Wacker. The Fair attracted more than 27 million visitors clearly demonstrating the lakefront's potential. Olmsted sculpted the shoreline into a landscape of islands, lagoons and promontories. The Exposition covers 600 acres and features nearly 200 neo-classic buildings.

1894
Ward pressures City Council to turn over the Lake Park lands to South Park Commission and stops Daniel Burnham's plans for a cultural campus in the park. Museums planned for that site, including the Field Museum of Natural History and the Adler Planetarium eventually are built on new landfill east of Illinois Central Railroad tracks and south of 12th Street.

1895
State Legislature prepares way for Lincoln Park Commission to expand the park to the north by granting it right to reclaim submerged lands along the lakeshore as far north as Devon Avenue.

1896
Precedent for Lake Shore Drive set when Commercial Club asks Daniel Burnham to present his plans for south lakefront.

1901
City transfers Lake Park to South Park Commission which names it Grant Park after 18th U.S. President, Ulysses S. Grant.

1905
South Shore Country Club, located at 71st Street and South Shore Drive, is founded as a suburban counterpart to urban clubs in Chicago, such as the Athletic Club. Original country club building is constructed that year. A theater is added in 1909, and the Club has horse riding events, tennis courts, a dining room and a pool, as well as hundreds of feet of beachfront.

1909
Burnham Plan published. Plan includes the idea for South Lake Shore Drive running through picturesque parks south from Grant Park through Jackson Park and north along the lake through Lincoln Park to the city limits: in effect, one continuous linear park. Burnham envisioned a city that would not only be efficient and attractive for its residents, but also so beautiful that it would draw visitors and commerce.

1909
Group of Chicago's civic-minded citizens, headed by Charles Henry Wacker, envisions a great outer drive system to relieve downtown traffic and skirt Michigan Avenue. Land is bought, drained and beautified. Sixteen hundred acres of lake shore begins to be filled in and North Michigan Boulevard is widened into four-lane local and four-lane express highway. To the south on filled land, a chain of drives are conceived to converge at city's center.

Boats in Jackson Park Yacht Harbor, 1921.
(Chicago Historical Society, ICHi-62339,
Photographer-Kaufmann & Fabry).

Sea Lion pond at Lincoln Park Zoo, 1889.
(Chicago Historical Society, ICHi-03463,
Photographer-unknown).

Area and Boundaries of Lincoln Park,
1873, from "A History of Lincoln Park,"
page 4 (1899).

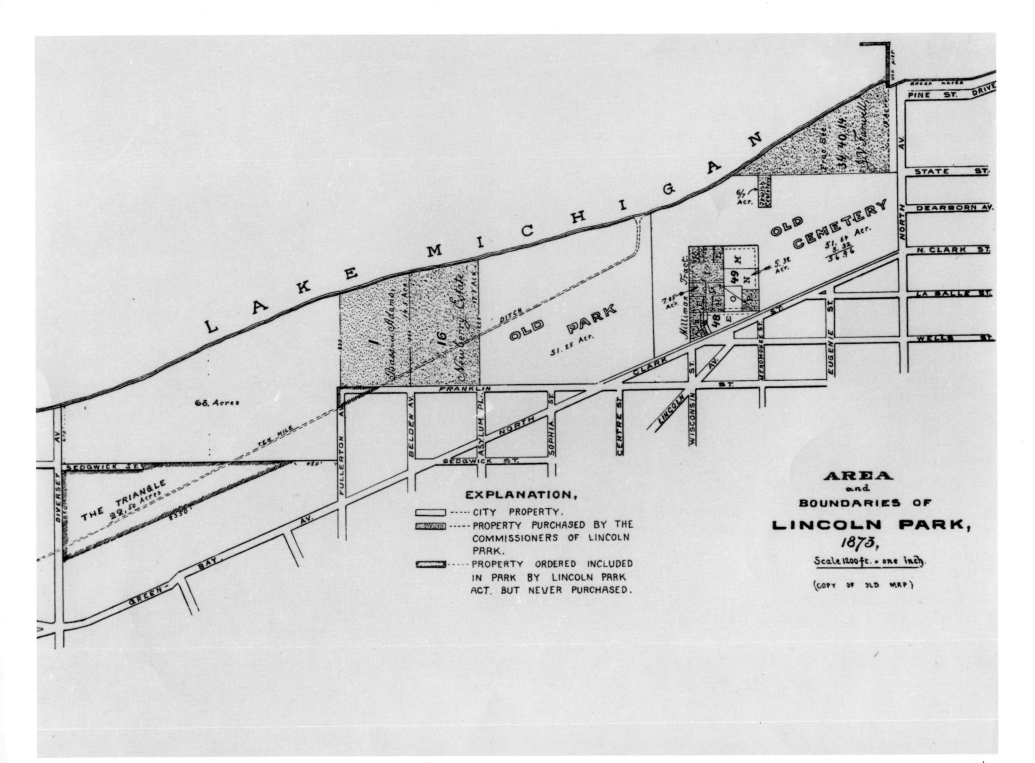

LAKE MICHIGAN

PINE ST. DRIVE
STATE ST.
DEARBORN AV.
N. CLARK ST.
LA SALLE ST.
WELLS ST.

OLD CEMETERY

OLD PARK
51.25 Acr.

THE TRIANGLE
22.50 Acres

60 Acres

EXPLANATION,

---- CITY PROPERTY.

---- PROPERTY PURCHASED BY THE
COMMISSIONERS OF LINCOLN
PARK.

---- PROPERTY ORDERED INCLUDED
IN PARK BY LINCOLN PARK
ACT. BUT NEVER PURCHASED.

AREA
and
BOUNDARIES OF
LINCOLN PARK,
1873,
Scale 1200 ft. = one inch.

(COPY OF OLD MAP)

R. H. McDONALD'S
MAP OF CHICAGO,
WITH A CORRECT OUTLINE OF THE
GREAT FIRE,
FROM A CAREFUL SURVEY BY SHARP & THAIN, OF CHICAGO.

NEW YORK:
R. B. THOMPSON & CO., Publishers,
125 BROADWAY.
1871.

CITY HALL.

D. LAMB,
PUBLISHER.

EXPLANATION:

City Limits
Parks and Boulevards
Railroads
Stations

RAILROADS.

	Depot No.
Atchison, Topeka & Santa Fe	6
Baltimore & Ohio	6
Chicago & Alton	3
Chicago & Erie	6
Chicago, Burlington & Quincy	3
Chicago Central	7
Chicago & Eastern Illinois	6
Chicago, Evanston & Lake Superior	3
Chicago & Grand Trunk	5
Chicago, Milwaukee & St. Paul	3
Chicago & Northern Pacific	7
Chicago & North-Western	2
Chicago, Rock Island & Pacific	4
Chicago, St. Paul & Kansas City	7
Chicago & Western Indiana	6
Illinois Central	6
Kankakee Line (C., C., C. & St. L.)	1
Lake Shore & Michigan Southern	4
Louisville, New Albany & Chicago	6
Michigan Central	1
New York, Chicago & St. Louis	4
Pittsburgh, Cincinnati, Chicago & St. Louis	
Pittsburgh, Fort Wayne & Chicago	3
Wabash	6
Wisconsin Central	7

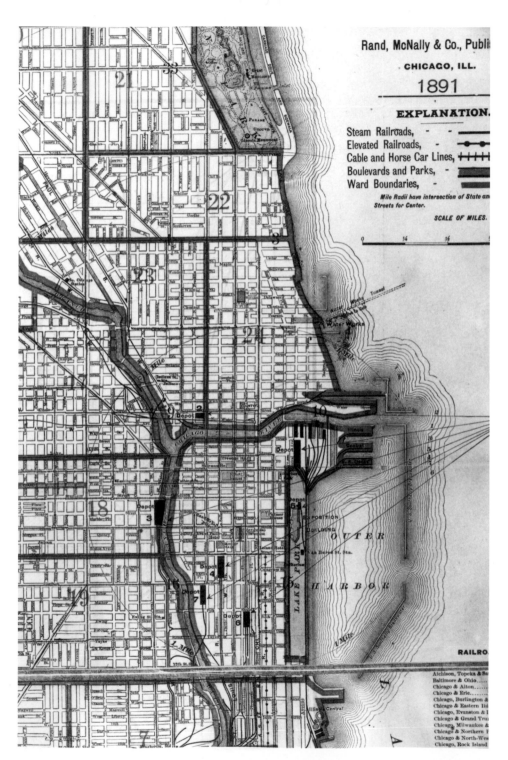

R. H. McDonald's "Map of Chicago, Great Fire." (Chicago Historical Society, ICHi-13511).

"Free Directory," Chicago, 1891, D. Lamb, Publisher. (Chicago Historical Society).

Rand McNally, Map of Chicago, 1891. (Chicago Historical Society).

TOM O'GORMAN | I think Lake Shore Drive has evolved into such an extraordinary emblematic piece of Chicago. It is the ultimate photograph of Chicago with the lake coming up and meeting the land. We owe much of this to Potter Palmer and it is just one more expression of his genius. He invented retail department store sales for Chicagoans, he invented good hotels in Chicago, and he had the ability to see that this was a key crossroads for the city. Of course, there was nothing there...it was horrible, it was swampy, there was no sand, everything was brought in and the actual drive itself was constructed only after he began the drive. The two big landowners who did that whole section of the Gold Coast in two triangles were the Catholic bishop of Chicago and Potter Palmer. Potter was on to something because once he had Henry Ives Cobb, the very young architect who was only 30 years old, and Charles Sumner Frost design this over-burdened tradition of a German Rhine castle. So, on the shores of Lake Michigan where there was nothing else as far as the eye could see, Palmer built this Prince Ludwig-style, "madman's" castle.

That turned the tide because all of his swanky friends from the South Side of the city from Prairie Avenue wanted a pied-a-terre on the North Side of the city... a townhouse like the wealthy had in England. I think that the Haymarket Riots had a lot to do with this because it spooked the big, important people who owned the houses on Prairie Avenue and wanted to go north to Lake Forest because next door to that city was Fort Sheridan. It meant that they would have troops at the ready to protect their property. So, now they wanted a big estate in Lake Forest and a townhouse that they could live at in the city. And, the amazing thing is that the same people who were building the large, exotic early Chicago skyscrapers also were the architects of these townhouses, including Burnham, Root, Sullivan, and Frank Lloyd Wright. They were very elegant townhouses and they were very modern. The people who lived on Prairie Avenue lived in these deep, heavy Victorian buildings that were filled with draperies and heavy, oppressive wood, and a lot of that kitschy stuff from the Victorian times. Once these townhouses started to be constructed in the Gold Coast, there was a doorway that opened to the modern because it was a new way of living that didn't need twenty servants.

However, at the Potter and Bertha Palmer mansion, when you arrived at their door and pressed the doorbell, if you handed your card to the butler that card would go through the hands of twenty-seven maids, butlers and social secretaries before it arrived on either Mrs. Palmer or Mr. Palmer's desk. That was how many servants they had in the house, and every servant would carry the card a few feet

Bertha Honore Palmer, about 1895. (Chicago Historical Society, Photographer-unknown).

Paved beach along lakefront in Lincoln Park showing High Bridge, ca. 1900. (Chicago Historical Society, ICHi-62341, Photographer-Frederick O. Bemm).

People along Jackson Park Beach, some standing in the water, 1908. (Chicago Historical Society, ICHi-62345, Photographer-George R. Lawrence).

to the next person, and it would go all the way up to where the Palmers were. The other interesting thing is that there were no doors in the Palmer mansion that had a door knob on the outside. A door always had to be opened by a servant and the house was honeycombed with interior passageways for the servants to move around.

I think that one of the greatest moments in the history of Lake Shore Drive came during the Columbian Exposition in 1893. Mrs. Palmer was a frequent visitor to all the great painting sites of the Impressionists, and their contemporaries and social equals in Chicago spent most of their time when they were invited to Palmer dinner parties squinting at the Impressionist paintings that filled the walls of their home. Those paintings were brand new to most Chicagoans, even the very wealthy ones. So, when they would go to the Palmer mansion, visitors would see these landscapes and seascapes or even just the flowers, they would be all out of focus and fuzzy to visitors unused to such art. There was no other place in Chicago where you could see these Impressionist painters except the Palmer home. So, Bertha Palmer was way ahead of her contemporaries with her French tastes (I believe that she was French by her own background since her maiden name was Honore).

She really reflected the extraordinary passions for the modern artists of that period in the late 1800s. Her collection is in the Art Institute of Chicago and the reason that there are more French Impressionists here than anywhere in the world, outside of the Musee de Dorsee in Paris, is because of Mrs. Palmer. She died in the early 1900s, and, really, her collection was the center of the Art Institute. She was the head of the Board of Women Managers to the World's Fair, and she was a tough person because she really ran the Fair. Her big issues besides the quality of the art, was that women be reflected very strongly. So Mary Cassett and other American women painters were at the focus of all of this. I say this because it is all connected to Lake Shore Drive. Lake Shore Drive was new and modern Chicago, not the old places on Prairie Avenue of old gentility...this was the new place.

A story that reflects that is worth telling. Thirty-two million people arrived to visit the World's Fair in 1893 during the six months that it was open. Among the visitors was Princess Eulalia, the official representative of the Queen Regent of Spain. She arrived with her entourage, and she was invited to the Palmer castle for a great dinner where all of Chicago society was to be present for the dinner. As she was leaving the Palmer House Hotel, where she had the royal suite, she turned to the U.S. Ambassador to Spain and said, "By the way, this is the Palmer House. The Palmers are no relation to the people with whom we are having dinner. Correct?" She was told, "Oh, yes. As a matter of fact that is who they are...

Pedestrians on lakefront walkway in Lincoln Park with excursion boats in background, ca. 1910. (Chicago Historical Society, ICHi-62335, Photographer-Casey Prunchunas.)

it is Mr. Palmer and his wife." She stopped dead in her tracks and she is reported to have said, "The Infanta of Spain does not eat with innkeepers." And, she refused to go to the dinner. As a result, there was much commotion among the U.S. Ambassador to Spain and the Spanish Ambassador to the U.S. who were trying to work out the situation. It was determined that she would pay a visit, but she would not eat in the house. At the house, Mrs. Palmer had a dais constructed by which the Infanta of Spain would never have to walk at the same level as other people. So, she was always elevated above them, even walking through the house there was a special pathway elevated for the Infanta of Spain. And, at the dinner she missed, the guests ate on solid gold dishware with solid gold utensils.

The press was all over the incident saying, "Spanish princess refuses to eat at the Palmer castle." But, Bertha Potter never uttered one single word about the incident, proving that she had more nobility than the Infanta. However, many years later, during the revolution in Spain and the Spanish royal family was thrown out of Spain for a while, the Infanta of Spain, who was much older by then, was living in Rome in exile. She wrote a note to Mrs. Palmer, who was visiting Rome, saying "The Infanta of Spain would like to invite Mrs. Palmer for tea." Mrs. Palmer responded with a note back that said, "Mrs. Palmer of Chicago does not take tea with the degenerate members of a bilious family." That was also all over the press in Chicago with four inch headlines– "Mrs. Palmer gets even with the Princess!" So, Bertha did demonstrate a new kind of social nobility very much different from that Edith Wharton-style in New York. You cannot talk about Lake Shore Drive without talking about the Palmers and their effect on it.

Potter Palmer's acquisition of the land for his house had a direct connection to Captain Streeter because when Palmer built his mansion in the 1880s, Streeter's property abutted the Gold Coast that was dominated by Palmer and his wealthy friends. The land that Palmer purchased was former Catholic cemetery property which was why the Archdiocese had all that property. It was the original property that had been purchased by the then Diocese of Chicago that they turned into a Catholic cemetery. As a tribute to President Abraham Lincoln, it was decided to build a park where all the cemeteries had been located, including non-denominational, Protestant, Jewish, and Catholic ones. They decided to move those bodies to appropriate cemeteries and then redo this land for a park named after Lincoln. So, they were doing that and many graves

Lincoln Park Stockton Drive, 1929. (Chicago Historical Society, DN-0088485, Photographer – Chicago Daily News).

following page
Michigan Avenue, north of Congress Street, 1890. (Chicago Historical Society, ICHi-20506, Photographer – Unknown).

Car and carriage on road in Lincoln Park, ca. 1915. (Chicago Historical Society, ICHi-62340, Photographer-Casey Prunchunas).

Suicide Bridge, Lincoln Park with policeman, ca. 1910. (Chicago Historical Society, ICHi-62353, Photographer-unknown).

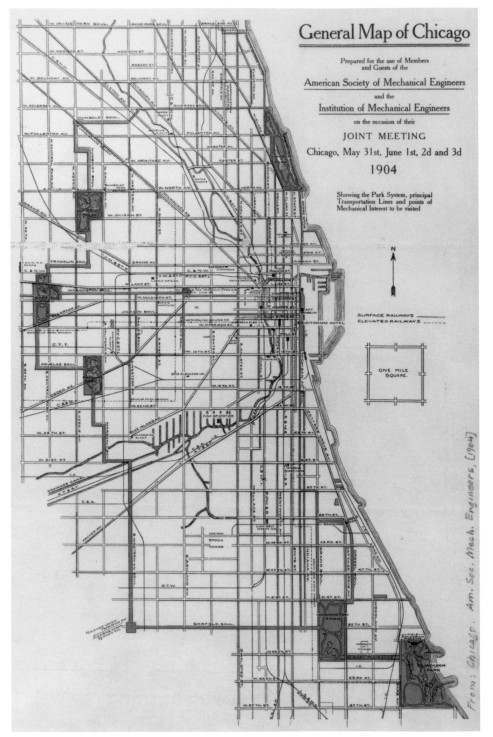

General Map of Chicago

Prepared for the use of Members
and Guests of the

American Society of Mechanical Engineers

and the

Institution of Mechanical Engineers

on the occasion of their

JOINT MEETING

Chicago, May 31st, June 1st, 2d and 3d

1904

Showing the Park System, principal
Transportation Lines and points of
Mechanical Interest to be visited

N

SURFACE RAILWAYS
ELEVATED RAILWAYS

ONE MILE
SQUARE.

From: Chicago. Am. Soc. Mech. Engineers, [1904]

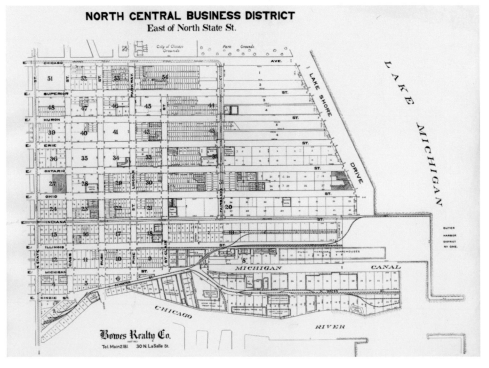

NORTH CENTRAL BUSINESS DISTRICT
East of North State St.

Bowes Realty Co.
Tel. Main 2181   30 N. LaSalle St.

General Map of Chicago, 1904, showing parks, principal transportation and mechanical points of interest, American Society of Mechanical Engineers. (Chicago Historical Society, ICHi-34343).

Monroe to Chicago Avenue, East of River, Map #3222, Ross and Company, 1923 (Chicago Historical Society, ICHi-29404).

North Central Business District, East of State Street, Bowes Realty Company. (Chicago Historical Society, ICHi-18443).

James Charnley Residence, 1204 Lake Shore Drive, ca. 1890. (Chicago Historical Society, ICHi-31157, Photographer-unknown).

Lake Michigan shore, view northeast from an observation tower and weather station on top of the Auditorium, 1907. (Chicago Historical Society, DN-0004926, Photographer–Chicago Daily News).

his wealthy friends. The land that Palmer purchased was former Catholic cemetery property which was why the Archdiocese had all that property. It was the original property that had been purchased by the then Diocese of Chicago that they turned into a Catholic cemetery. As a tribute to President Abraham Lincoln, it was decided to build a park where all the cemeteries had been located, including non-denominational, Protestant, Jewish, and Catholic ones. They decided to move those bodies to appropriate cemeteries and then redo this land for a park named after Lincoln. So, they were doing that and many graves had been removed in October, 1871 when the Great Chicago Fire happened. The Fire burned from Roosevelt Road on the south to Fullerton (the city's northern boundary) on the north, but there were many people on the far northern end of the Fire who dove into the empty graves to let the fire pass over them. And, the Fire did go on to the end of Lincoln Park to Fullerton. The bodies of Roman Catholics were supposed to be moved and sent to Evanston to Calgary Cemetery, but that was only partially true.

In 1880, after the Chicago Fire, the Catholic population of the city was growing so fast here that they made Chicago an Archdiocese. They brought in a foreign-born, Irish heroic priest from St. Louis named Patrick Augustine Feehan, and made him the first Archbishop of Chicago. In anticipation of the first archbishop living in the city, Pashley, the architect, designed that big old red brick Queen Anne house with all the chimneys on North Avenue and State Street near Lake Shore Drive. I believe that the lawn that the Cardinal's house sits on today is filled with bodies from the old cemetery that were not moved in the 1800s.

I don't know if the Catholic Church gave Potter Palmer the land where he built his mansion, and I think that he may have been shrewd enough to buy the land. He was making radical changes after the Fire, and the Catholic Church would have acquired that land back in the 1840s. I think that there were actually two Catholic cemeteries, one pre-1850 and one post-1850. I think that the one under the lawn at the Cardinal's house was pre-1850. Palmer wanted Lake Shore Drive in front of his mansion because he wanted to have the carriages of the elites drive by his house.

Most of the McCormicks lived in "McCormickville" near Rush Street at Erie. There were also McCormick mansions on Lake Shore Drive. The great thing is that once Palmer anchored the Gold Coast with his "castle" then the area took off and people wanted to be there, including Abraham Lincoln's son, Robert Todd. The Gold Coast residents were always very close, extremely social, and they all contributed to the city's artistic life. I think that the children of the first great entrepreneurs were really into the arts.

Horse and surrey on wide road in Lincoln Park, ca. 1899. (Chicago Historical Society, ICHi-62346, Photographer-unknown).

View of unpaved Lake Shore Drive at
Ulysses S. Grant memorial at left, ca. 1890.
(Chicago Historical Society, ICHi-62382,
Photographer-unknown).

Looking south on Lake Shore Drive, April,
1891. (Chicago Historical Society, ICHi-25684,
Photographer-unknown).

Jackson Park Beach with refectory pavilion in
background, 1892. (Chicago Historical Society,
ICHi-14852, Photographer-unknown).

13283

RICHARD WARD | Apparently Lake Shore Drive began back with Potter Palmer who got the city to build the initial stretch up north that went by his house which increased the value of his property and his access. That was really the start of having a road on the lakefront.

I think that the stimulus and catalyst for keeping the lakefront open was probably Montgomery Ward for a very limited stretch of land in which he had an interest. His headquarters was on the northwest corner of Madison and Michigan Avenues, and his office looked out across Grant Park, and the "park" was a mess in 1890. He got his general counsel at Montgomery Ward to research what the legal protections were for Grant Park, and, in 1890, they filed their first lawsuit in what has become known as the Ward Decisions. The argument that they had was the Dedication Restrictions of 1836 that were effective between Madison and 11th Street. It wasn't Roosevelt Road, because there were already buildings constructed at 11th Street that extended out east of Michigan Avenue.

There were four Illinois Supreme Court decisions related to the Montgomery Ward suits. In 1897, the court eventually decided that the area to be protected was from the west side of Michigan Avenue out to the Illinois Central Railroad tracks that had originally been constructed in the lake, but by 1897 the land had already been filled in and there was Lake Park located there out to the lake. The railroad tracks had originally been erected 400 feet into the lake from the west side of Michigan Avenue, and the IC was allowed a 300 foot stretch where they were allowed to construct a trestle in around 1852. Then they had to fill in everything under the trestle because what Chicago wanted was a breakwater.

During the years between 1850 and the Chicago Fire, in 1871, the Lake Park lake had been filled in and the final small portion that had remained as a lake was then filled in with debris from the Fire. So, when Montgomery Ward filed his first lawsuit in 1890, he was trying to protect the land out to the railroad trestle and wasn't really looking beyond it. He won that lawsuit in 1897. The next thing that happened was they realized that the court decision was only controlling out to the Illinois Central Railroad tracks, and they decided to build the Armory east of the railroad because the Illinois Supreme Court decision wasn't applicable there. But Ward sued again and that case was decided in 1901, and, again, Ward won the second decision because the Court ruled that the Dedication Restrictions are extended out as you add to either natural or manmade land. So, if you add anything to the lakefront, the Dedication Restrictions follow it out. And the city couldn't build the Armory east of the railroad tracks.

View of Brewster residence at 1220 North
Lake Shore Drive, ca. 1911. (Chicago Historical
Society, ICHi-62372, Photographer-unknown).

O.W. Potter residence, 130 Lake Shore Drive,
1893. (Chicago Historical Society, ICHi-62352,
Photographer-unknown).

Then, Chicago gave the land to the South Park Commissioners because they figured they would give it to a different governmental body. They even got the state legislature to pass legislation to allow museums in parks because, by that time, they wanted to build the Field Museum out where Buckingham Fountain is now located, right in the middle of Grant Park. So, Ward filed his third lawsuit and he won that one in about 1909. The Illinois Supreme Court said that it is legal to build a museum in a park, but not a park that is protected by a Dedication Restriction against buildings and any obstructions whatsoever. So that didn't work for those who wanted to build the Field Museum out where the Buckingham Fountain is now.

But, the city said, they had the power of eminent domain. Ward did his homework and filed his fourth lawsuit and it went through the courts and, in 1911, the Illinois Supreme Court handed down its judgment on his suit. They said that the power of eminent domain can be utilized only for legal purposes and it would be illegal to violate the conditions of the covenant or the Dedication Restrictions. So, the court said that the city could not use the power of eminent domain to trump the Dedication Restrictions. In fact, the court made it even harder when it said that the Illinois legislature could not violate the Dedication Restrictions.

In 1890, when Montgomery Ward filed his first lawsuit, the Art Institute had not been envisioned at that time. The idea to build the Art Institute happened in 1891 when the lawsuit had already been filed. By that time, Ward had become very unpopular, and when he looked out his window at Madison and Michigan, he saw that what they wanted to build was a very limited building on Michigan Avenue that would only have a frontage of 400 feet. He figured that because of the location and dimensions, that would be as far east as they could build the museum out to the railroad. Since he was so unpopular by that time, he decided not to amend his lawsuit in 1892, and he left out the Art Institute in his complaint. Ironically, the Art Institute has expanded to over seven times the originally approved area since 1892. The museum has been challenged a couple of times, including one time for filing too late. So, effectively, there have been no real exceptions to the Ward Decisions, decided by the Illinois Supreme Court.

This is a very unique area in that it has a three-level roadway system. In the city's early years, west of Michigan Avenue, Wacker Drive was a mess and it was used for unloading ships, buggy traffic, and pedestrian traffic. On the east side of Michigan Avenue were railroad tracks. When they began to develop the Illinois Central Railroad area, the double-roadway system that was west of Michigan Avenue was extended across and over to the east side of Michigan Avenue. On the west side they had Upper Wacker Drive and Lower Wacker Drive, and when they extended across to the east they wanted to have the same upper and lower Wacker Drives. They named the third railroad level as Lower Lower Wacker.

Interstate Industrial Exposition Building, late 1880s. (Chicago Historical Society, ICHi-02173, Photographer-J.W. Taylor).

CHAPTER 2
IMPLEMENTATION OF THE BURNHAM PLAN 1909–1930s

1911
After four contentious lawsuits, Ward is triumphant when the Illinois Supreme Court declares that the original designation of the downtown lakefront as "forever open, clear and free of buildings" was an iron-clad prohibition against the construction of permanent buildings in Grant Park, with the exception of the Art Institute.

1915
Jackson Park Pavilion (63rd Street Beach House) was built (reconstructed in 1999).

1916
Edgewater Beach Hotel opens on lake at Sheridan near Foster with 400 luxurious rooms.

1916
South Shore Country Club hires Marshall and Fox to design a new clubhouse in Mediterranean Revival style. Originally built as a Protestant-only club, Catholics later were admitted.

1919
Soldier Field designed.

1919
Burnham Plan inspires Chicago City Council to pass lakefront ordinance calling for construction on a series of islands, parks, lagoons and beaches along with a new sports stadium on the lakefront. Illinois Central Railroad cooperates by electrifying and depressing its tracks on the South Side.

1920
Drake Hotel is built at Lake Shore Drive, Oak Street and Michigan Avenue by John and Tracy Drake. It becomes one of the nation's first urban resorts.

1921
New landfill abutting south end of Grant Park permits construction of Field Museum of Natural History.

1924
Sports stadium opens on October 9 and is named Municipal Grant Park Stadium.

1925
Municipal Grant Park Stadium renamed Soldier Field on November 11 in honor of American war veterans.

1926
Soldier Field formally dedicated on November 27 during 29th Army-Navy game.

1927
Edgewater Beach Apartments built nearby hotel.

1927
Link between Grant and Jackson Parks officially named Burnham Park. It is located along Lake Michigan from Roosevelt Road to 56th Street, including Promontory Point.

1927
Clarence Buckingham Fountain commissioned by Kate Buckingham to honor her late brother.

1929
Northerly Island created out of landfill.

1930
Burnham Park construction completed. South Lake Shore Drive opened between Grant Park and Jackson Park.

1930
New landfill permits construction of Adler Planetarium and John G. Shedd Aquarium.

Cars on road in northern extension of
Lincoln Park, August 11, 1916.
(Chicago Historical Society, ICHi-62334,
Photographer-Hornby & Freiberg).

View along lakefront in Lincoln Park, taken off high bridge showing people and car, 1913. (Chicago Historical Society, ICHi-62332, Photographer-unknown).

Michigan Avenue and Grant Park, looking east across Illinois Central Railroad tracks, c. 1920s. (Chicago Historical Society, Photographer-unknown).

Michigan Avenue looking north from Congress Hotel, showing Art Institute building on right, 1908. (Chicago Historical Society, ICHi-62331, Photographer-George R. Lawrence).

PHOTO BY
THE GEO. R. LAWRENCE CO.
CHICAGO

BLAIR KAMIN | I have never been on a more beautiful urban highway than Lake Shore Drive. It is attractive because it isn't a highway, at least in spirit. It's a boulevard, particularly with the plantings and the trees that Mayor Richard M. Daley has put in since he took office in 1989. What really makes it beautiful, though, is that it's the classic condition that architects call an "edge" and there's this cliff of skyscrapers, particularly on the North Side and downtown. And, Lake Shore Drive slices through, so, it is a very dynamic experience particularly when you come up from the south, past Soldier Field and the Museum Campus, and this wall of skyscrapers just explodes right in front of you and takes your breath away. The same thing happens when you come around the "S" curve towards Oak Street because, again, you see this incredible range of residential apartment buildings extending northward like a mountain range all the way up through Lincoln Park. Because it's a boulevard and not a highway, there aren't any trucks. You have beautiful art deco medians that the city put in during the Daley administration along with beautiful trees and beautiful landscaping. So, that softens the experience, somewhat.

If you have ever looked closely at the road itself in certain places on the north and southbound sides of it, in many cases the separated lanes are not on the same plane. Clearly, the intent of the engineers was to relieve the sense of a vast, continuous stretch of asphalt. They wanted to make it more comfortable so that you weren't just looking at a guy in a car right across the way. Instead, you were looking at beautiful trees, or you were raised above those cars across the way so that you actually had a view out to the water. It is not just the city you are looking at, but also the water, and the incredible contrast between the two and that enriches your experience. On one hand you have density, power, what man has made, and, on the other, you have what is natural and just this incredibly placid or roaring expanse of water. So, it is amazing.

For all its beauty, Lake Shore Drive is a big and intimidating barrier for pedestrians who want to get from the city to the water. It is as wide as a ten-lane highway, and when you combine it on the South Side with the Illinois Central Railroad tracks, which are every bit as wide and right next to it you have enormous distance for people to cover. It is as big as three or four football fields, and maybe more to get from city to water. My predecessor, Paul Gapp, a wonderful man and wonderful writer, called this phenomenon a concrete curtain, like the Iron Curtain, and it is still a problem to this very day.

The city has made some strides in creating better pedestrian access.

Cars in front of boathouse in Jackson Park
lakefront, ca. 1915. (Chicago Historical Society,
ICHi-62338, Photographer-unknown).

For example, there is a sky lit tunnel between Grant Park and the Museum Campus. There are plans—which have been sitting there for six or seven years—for pedestrian bridges on the South Side. There have been some tunnels done, such as the one between the Museum of Science and Industry and the 57th Street beach. But nonetheless, the Drive and the IC tracks, in particular, are a huge barrier.

There are people in Milwaukee who think they have a pretty nice urban roadway along their lakefront, too. They look at Chicago and they say, "Oh, my God, we've got this nice little two or three lane highway along our lakefront and you guys have this expressway." Well, it isn't really an expressway, but it can be close to that with people driving 60 miles an hour and ignoring the speed limit.

I think that it wasn't just the roadway but it was Daniel Burnham's vision that prevented the lakefront from being another Cleveland with all kinds of factories and other junk along it like the wharves in New York City. Burnham clearly looked at the lakefront as a place for recreation and culture, not commerce and industry. He was incredibly shrewd and sold this to the businessmen because at the same time he was taking money out of their pockets—no factories and no shipping—he was saying that this will enrich you and your city. It will make your city beautiful, it will be prestigious, and it will be a great place for real estate. And, you know what? He was right. Lake Shore Drive is a prestigious address. It's beautiful, and it combines commerce and culture, all in one. It is a rare win-win.

Burnham's vision was for a continuous chain of parks stretching from the Indiana border not just to Evanston, but all the way north to Wilmette. Part of that was a linear road because how else are you going to get there? Even in 1909 when the Burnham Plan came out, people had to get there somehow and there had to be a road. Well, it wasn't going to be just any road, it was going to be a beautiful boulevard that was comparable to something out of Paris which was the inspiration, the end-all and be-all for everything that Burnham designed. So, I think the road and the parks go together. They are part of this vision for a civilized edge that wouldn't just benefit private interests but public interests and the people as a whole.

View looking north on Lake Shore Drive from Drake Hotel, with view of Oak Street, ca 1920. (Chicago Historical Society, Photographer–unknown).

following page
Two men fishing from rowboat in Jackson Park lagoon, ca. 1915. (Chicago Historical Society, ICHi-62337, Photographer-unknown).

Excursion boat "Ivanhoe" along lakefront in Lincoln Park, 1899. (Chicago Historical Society, ICHi-62347, Photographer-unknown).

Family in rowboat in Lincoln Park, ca. 1913. (Chicago Historical Society, ICHi-62334, Photographer-Casey Prunchunas.)

View of cars on Lake Shore Drive just West of Field Museum, showing skyline, pedestrian bridge and double-decker bus, 1934. (Chicago Historical Society, ICHi-62379, Photographer-unknown).

View of Lake Shore Drive looking
north from Drake Hotel, 1926.
(Chicago Historical Society, ICHi-14143,
Photographer-Kaufmann & Fabry Co.).

Lake Shore Drive, north from Oak Street,
1928. (Chicago Historical Society, ICHi-04326,
Photographer-Kaufmann & Fabry).

The Stevens Hotel with Field museum in background, under construction on August 25, 1925. (Courtesy of Robert V. Allegrini).

Completed Stevens Hotel with Field museum in background. (Courtesy of Robert V. Allegrini).

View of second Palmer House looking west on Monroe Street, ca. early 1900s. (Courtesy of Robert V. Allegrini).

Drake Hotel at Michigan and
Lake Shore Drive, early 1920s, looking north.
(Courtesy of Robert V. Allegrini).

The Stevens Hotel, soon after opening in 1927.
(Courtesy of Robert V. Allegrini).

The Drake Hotel, as seen in postcard, c. 1930.
(Courtesy of Robert V. Allegrini).

View of cars on Outer Drive (Lake Shore Drive) showing skyline, 1925. (Chicago Historical Society, ICHi-62375, Photographer-unknown).

Two workers standing next to a wall in a construction site in Grant Park, 1928. (Chicago Historical Society, DN-0066473, Photographer-Chicago Daily News).

Automobiles driving over a bridge on a
new drive north of Fullerton Avenue in the
Lincoln Park community area, 1927.
(Chicago Historical Society, DN-0082552,
Photographer Chicago Daily News).

Rear view of Frederick D. Countiss residence at 1524 Lake Shore Drive, with parked car, ca. 1920. (Chicago Historical Society, ICHi-62383, Photographer-unknown).

East Lake Shore Drive, July, 1924. (Chicago Historical Society, ICHi-25681, Photographer-unknown).

Lake Shore Drive looking south from
Oak Street, 1915. (Chicago Historical Society,
ICHi-19834, Photographer–unknown).

Stockton Drive in Lincoln Park, 1921.
(Chicago Historical Society, ICHi-03451,
Photographer-unknown).

Birdseye view of crowds in Grant Park for Decoration Day, May, 1889. (Chicago Historical Society, ICHi-62370, Photographer-unknown).

Outer Drive bridge and view of harbor and
University of Illinois at Navy Pier, ca 1950.
(Chicago Historical Society, ICHi-00157,
Photographer-Don Honick).

South Shore Country Club,
7059 South Shore Drive, 1936.
(Chicago Historical Society, ICHi-62494,
Photographer-unknown).

CHAPTER 3
CENTURY OF PROGRESS AND EXPANSION OF OUTER AND INNER DRIVES 1933–1946

1933
Century of Progress Exposition takes place along lakefront on hundreds of acres of landfill adjacent to southern border of Grant Park. It opens on May 27, 1933 and closes in 1934. Of that landfill, Northerly Island eventually becomes Meigs Field, and other parts will one day be McCormick Place. Additional parkland is created between 12th and 39th Streets.

1933
North Lake Shore Drive, also known as the Outer Drive, is extended from Belmont to Foster Avenue.

1935
The vast Lake Shore Drive project, costing an estimated $100 million is completed, except for vital point across the Chicago River.

1937
On October 18 when President Franklin Delano Roosevelt dedicates the last connecting roadway link between the North and South Side Outer Drives. The "S" curve connection was built across the river and above the rail yards and industrial areas below. The roadway bridge's main span across the river was a $2.9 million, double-decker, bascule-style bridge dubbed Centennial Bridge. At the time it opened, it was the longest and widest bascule bridge in the world. The lower level of the bridge was intended for a railroad connection but was never used until the road was rebuilt in 1986. Two northbound lanes of South Lake Shore Drive were named after Leif Erikson and the two southbound lanes were named after Christopher Columbus.

1939
New Outer Drive, built on the filled lakefront, completed up to North Avenue.

1942
New Outer Drive extended north to Belmont Avenue and south to 42nd Street.

View of cars on Outer Drive at Foster Avenue,
June, 1949. (Chicago Historical Society,
ICHi-62378, Photographer-Dr. Frank E. Rice.

POTTER PALMER | I remember, as a kid, about my great grandfather and grandmother, Potter and Bertha Palmer's castle on Lake Shore Drive. When I was young, the interior of the castle had furniture that was covered with sheets, whenever I went into the place. I think that the last time that anyone had lived there was just before the Depression, and it was opened one other time for my Aunt Pauline's debut party in the late 1930s. But, other than that, it was just shut down and there was nobody living inside the mansion. However, there was a garage just to the west of the castle itself, and that was where my grandmother's chauffeur kept the cars and washed them every day.

We used to go to the castle when I was a kid and played a game called "guns." If you look at the pictures of the castle you will see that the building was filled with little nooks and crannies, and somebody would start out and go hide somewhere. Then, somebody else would try to find them. Since we would carry wooden guns or cap pistols, the minute you saw the other person you would yell out "bang, I've killed you!" So, we used to do that. Then, later on, because we outgrew the game quite quickly, we used to play baseball on the part of the lawn located just north of the old castle itself. As we got bigger and stronger, and could hit the ball out onto Schiller Street we needed a better place to play ball.

There was also a tennis court on the property, and, once in a while, people would come back and play tennis. I never knew who they were. They were just local people, I guess. Nobody would stop them. They would just come and play tennis.

I never saw the castle in operation so I didn't know that there had been many butlers and maids working there. We never really talked much about when my great grandmother and great grandfather lived there. I am guessing, and I don't know this as a fact, that my grandmother and grandfather moved in after my great grandmother died sometime around 1920. But, I never saw it in operation. I can remember being in the castle a couple of times with the furniture covered with sheets so it wouldn't get all dusty. As for when it was torn down, the story that I believed to be true although it came from hearsay but was passed around the family, was that we sold the castle to a man named Mr. Bendix in the 1930s. But, we had to take the mortgage back as a partial payment, and after he defaulted on that, we took the castle back in the family. Then, it was sold to developers right after WW II and torn down sometime in the late 1940s. Two rental apartment buildings were constructed on that block along Lake Shore Drive.

Aerial view of South Shore Drive during relocation, May 23, 1953. (Chicago Historical Society, ICHi-62326, Photographer-Calvin C. Oleson).

Night Scene at Michigan and Adams with Straus Building beacon, 1929. (Chicago Historical Society, ICHi-52041, Photographer-Kaufmann & Fabry Co.).

View south on Lake Shore Drive at the curve, Oak Street beach at lower mid, Palmolive Building and the Drake Hotel at mid-right. (Chicago Historical Society, ICHi-20912, Photographer–unknown).

Aerial view of northern end of Lake Shore Drive, including Edgewater Beach Hotel and landfill at Foster Avenue, c. 1950. (Chicago Historical Society, Photographer–unknown).

Bridge over Chicago River connecting Lake Shore Drive at "S" curve. (Chicago Historical Society, Photographer–unknown).

Lake Shore Drive "S" Curve, February 6, 1956.
(Chicago Historical Society, ICHi-34531,
Photographer-unknown).

Aerial view of downtown, Lake Shore
Drive "S" curve, looking west from lake,
c. 1930s. (Chicago Historical Society,
Photographer-unknown).

Birdseye view of Lincoln Park looking north,
ca. 1950. (Chicago Historical Society).

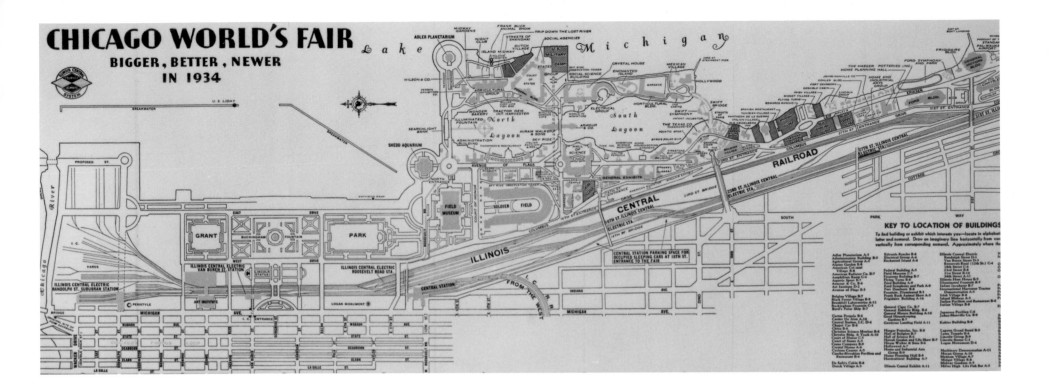

Century of Progress, Travel and Transportation Building, 1933-34. (Chicago Historical Society, ICHi-19901, Photographer – unknown).

Century of Progress, Rand McNally, 1934. (Chicago Historical Society, ICHi-02085, Photographer – unknown).

CHAPTER 4
LAKE SHORE DRIVE DEVELOPED FROM NORTH TO SOUTH 1946–1987

1946
Outer Drive officially renamed
Lake Shore Drive.

1955
 Drive extended from Foster to Hollywood.
Landfill used for extension includes rubble and
debris from homes and factories razed for
the construction of Congress Expressway, now
known as the Eisenhower Expressway.

1960
McCormick Place, the lakeside convention
center, opens.

1966
New Comprehensive Plan of Chicago notes
that "the Lake Michigan shoreline is a priceless
natural and man-made asset for the entire region.
It is the most important single recreational
resource in the metropolitan area and has been
a special concern to citizens, planners and
public officials through the city's history."

1967
McCormick Place burns down.

1967
Edgewater Beach Hotel closes.

1971
New McCormick Place opens.

1971
Aliotta, Haynes and Jeremiah singing group
record Lake Shore Drive.

1975
South Shore Country Club liquidates its assets
and property is sold to Chicago Park District for
$9,775,000. Facility is renovated and eventually
named the South Shore Cultural Center.

1982
Wacker Drive is extended east from Michigan
Avenue to meet Drive at the"S" curve.
Construction begins on a re-configuration of
the "S" curve in which the Drive, from Monroe
Street to Wacker Drive, is rerouted along new
lake landfill to greatly reduce the sharpness
of the curve. New parkland road south of
Randolph is named the Cancer Survivor's Plaza.

1986
Expansion of McCormick Place opened.

1987
New Lake Shore Drive without "S" curve
opens along with a lower level connection to
Wacker Drive.

North Lake Shore Drive at night with cars driving toward Drake Hotel and Oak Street. (Courtesy of Eric Bronsky Collection).

BLAIR KAMIN | The Drive and the parks were gradually expanded, and the Hollywood extension was done in the 1950s. There has been talk, here and there, in recent years about extending it up to Evanston. Well, the people in those God-awful high rises on Sheridan Road think this is like the hordes are going to come in and destroy their private backyards. So, there is intense political opposition in Edgewater and Rogers Park.

On the South Side, why does the Drive stop around 71st Street near the South Side Cultural Center? That is the forgotten part of Chicago that is now an overwhelmingly black and Hispanic area but let's hope that changes. We have this new plan for the ole U.S. Steel South Works that envisions widening the Drive as it goes further south for a few blocks from 79th to 83rd Streets to promote access. These things come incrementally and they don't all happen at once. That would be fantastic if it were to happen because that would really connect that area, which presently might as well be in Siberia, to the downtown.

I think that the south lakefront, in particular, has that quality of looking back on to the city because it juts out further to the east into the lake and so you really do see that change in the skyline. It is one of the reasons that the South Side is still an undiscovered jewel and that includes Burnham Park and Rainbow Beach, as well.

Being on the Drive is a very American experience. Americans are restless, they like to drive, they like to move, and they don't like to stick in one place. So, here is a kind of pleasure that is elicited not from strolling in the Gardens of Versailles. It is in a way more democratic. Anybody who is going through the park that Daniel Burnham envisioned and along the road that he envisioned can get this majestic vision that is fit for a king, but it is available for everyone. The lakefront is ennobling to the city. People have criticized Burnham for not paying enough attention to the neighborhoods, but everybody, sooner or later, winds up on Lake Shore Drive if you are in the city of Chicago.

It is this kind of linear path that connects north and south, poor and rich, and it is quite a way to travel because of all that it offers us, including water, skyline, and a swath of green. If you mix those three things together as you are driving along, it is an intensely rich experience and it is also always changing because of the perspective in the road. There are curves, you come around a bend, you do this, you do that, you are trying to avoid the traffic jam at the Oak Street curve, or you are stuck between Roosevelt and Chicago where you are always jammed up at rush hour. But the view is incomparable and you know that there are million dollar views wherever you look.

South Shore Drive, ca 1950.
(Chicago Historical Society, DN-0088472,
Photographer–Chicago Daily News).

The Conrad Hilton looking north
down Michigan Avenue, 1960s.
(Courtesy of Robert V. Allegrini)

There is a direct conflict between Lake Shore Drive's identity as a U.S. highway and a major urban arterial, and its identity as the way to get to all these great parks along the lakefront. What is a highway? A highway is a way to get quickly from point A to point B. That identity means speeding cars. Yes, there are no trucks, but you have all these cars whipping down the lakefront at 50 miles an hour. That is in complete conflict with the identity of pedestrians ambling slowly from their neighborhoods or even from downtown to the water's edge where it is supposed to be serene and peaceful.

If you ever just stand at the eastern edge of Grant Park, what do you hear? Do you hear lapping waters, screeching gulls, the rigging of sails gentling tingling? No, what you hear is cars racing along as if you were at Daytona Raceway. It is like being on the Dan Ryan Expressway because you have people driving like "bats out of hell" so that they can get from the North Side to the South Side, or vice versa. That's the conflict of the lakefront right there, between the park and the road.

Lake Shore Drive has a huge impact on Grant Park. In theory, Grant Park is Versailles, an American version of the Gardens of Versailles. It is symmetrical, it is classical, it is this axis of Congress Parkway running through it right into Buckingham Fountain. That was the center of the Burnham Plan. It is as though,

on a larger scale, we have transported the Gardens of Versailles to the meeting of the Great Plains and the Great Lakes. Well, that sounds majestic and powerful, but, in reality these gardens are sliced and diced by all these roads that cut right through them. What are the roads doing? They are providing a connection between Lake Shore Drive, one highway, to another highway, the Congress Parkway, and from it to all the other highways, so you get Jackson and Balbo and Monroe, and, worst of all Columbus, which, in itself is like an eight-lane highway. And, there are these giant slices of asphalt cutting through this formal park, which is supposed to be like Versailles. It is only when there is a special event in Grant Park, and the roads are closed, like Taste of Chicago, the Pope comes to Chicago, the Bulls win a championship, the Art Institute's Modern Wing opens, that these roads are temporarily closed. And it ticks off drivers to no end because their access routes are slowed down.

But, only then does the park really fulfill its potential as a great space. It becomes more like Central Park where Frederick Law Olmsted very shrewdly created subterranean park drives that were below the surface of the parkland, and, thus maintain the continuity of this urban pleasure ground that he was creating. But, that doesn't happen in Grant Park. There is no respect for continuity. It's very

"Chicago," very pragmatic. Slice the road right through it. Sorry, too bad!

When Columbus Drive cut through the northern end of Grant Park, initially nobody cared because, to the east of Columbus Drive, you had Daley Bicentennial Plaza, and, to the west, you didn't have Millennium Park, the Bean, the Frank Gehry Band Shell, or the fountain. You had a parking lot and you had a bunch of working commuter railroad tracks, this gash that had been in the middle of Grant Park ever since the city was developed. When Daniel Burnham did the 1909 Plan, he assumed that those railroad trackswould stay and he didn't try to cover them over with anything. So, the point is that there was no real concern about people moving from Michigan Avenue to the water, from west to east, and vice versa at the north end. And when you look at Daley Bicentennial Plaza, in its original design from the 1970s, all of the motion is from Randolph Street, south to Buckingham Fountain, north to south, not east to west.

Well, now we have Millennium Park and a way was needed to get from Millennium Park to Daley Bicentennial Plaza, and then to the waterfront. That is why you have that snaking, Frank Gehry-designed, BP Bridge there because then the east-west motion becomes important, getting from the city to the water and back and forth becomes very important. Before Millennium Park no one really questioned why that giant roadway—Columbus Drive—was there and what it was doing to the park.

ABNER MIKVA | I would absolutely agree with the premise of your working title that Lake Shore Drive is Urban America's Most Beautiful Roadway. It could never be built today because the environmentalists, including me, would be all over anybody who would try to plan to take this much lakefront and put it into a highway. It is a major transportation road/highway and always has been. But, I am so glad it is there because it sets off the lakefront, and it sets off the city in a special way. I don't know of any other city that has anything like this.

I have travelled all over the world and seen other cities that have beachfronts and lakefronts that are beautiful. But, I just love to be able to drive down it, and you look in one direction and see this glorious lake and its expansion that goes on forever. Then you look in the other direction and there is this wonderful city full of tall, tall buildings and you see the wonderful skyline and the lake, and it is almost a picture book scene.

Part of Chicago's history was that we really grew from the lake. The original settlements and the original housing were along the lake, as well as the Loop.

Other cities located on lakes don't quite have that history. For example, Detroit grew outward rather than spreading north and south along the lakefront, and I think that Cleveland is the same way. We literally grew north and south along the lake, and everyone hugged the lake. The first really great living areas were south and north of the Chicago River. To the south, the rich people who lived in Kenwood and, later on, moved to Hyde Park. And, the rich people who lived north went all the way up to the suburbs.

In fact, I grew up in Milwaukee, and, I remember, at that time, it was before the super highways, we used to come down U.S. 41 which came southward along the lake from Wisconsin. And, we would go through these beautiful suburban areas with huge estates on them and then come into the city on Lake Shore Drive, which was the entry to the city.

It was very gratifying and exciting to end up representing that whole area of the North Shore. And, earlier, I represented the South Side all the way out to Hegewisch and Calumet City, much of it along Lake Shore Drive. I represented areas as far west as Park Ridge, on the north, and as far west as Beverly, on the south, but both districts mostly hugged the shoreline. Important lakefront areas were Evanston, on the north, and, Hyde Park and South Shore on the south.

East Lake Shore Drive from Oak Street, 1926.
(Chicago Historical Society, ICHi-25683,
Photographer-Kaufman & Fabry).

Those were the areas where most of my voters lived and the basis of most of my support.

When I was a U.S. Congressman representing Hyde Park, it was always such a nice feeling when I would drive along the Drive. There were almost no buildings east of the Drive coming from the south, so I would look at the lake out of my right hand car window, and I would look at the skyline coming up out of my left hand window, and I just felt that I had the best of all possible windows. I loved the lake and grew up on it in Milwaukee and here in Chicago. So, the idea of being able to see the lake all the way downtown and then look at all of these huge office buildings, one of which was going to swallow me up for the day in my little office. Although I was going to be an indoor person, there always was the lake and wonderful Lake Shore Drive that I could take coming home.

I remember taking my eldest daughter, Mary, to see the sunrise early one morning when she was 5 or 6 years old and we were living in Hyde Park. She had either expressed some interest in it or I had thought that it was a teaching moment. We sat on the beach at 57th Street and watched the sun come up and it was a great sunrise. She was very excited about it. So, a few weeks later, we went to the Dunes in Michigan, which is on the other side of the lake, and she thought it

Aerial View of Lake Shore Drive "S" Curve,
ca 1950 (Chicago Historical Society,
ICHi-23469, Photographer–unknown).

Aerial view of South Lake Shore Drive with
Field Museum, Soldier Field and McCormick
Place, c. 1990. (Courtesy of The Walsh Group)

would be great to show her younger sister, who was obviously her pupil on everything, what the sunrise looked like. So, she made Laurie get up about five o'clock in the morning and they sat there. And, they sat and they sat and they sat, and the sun didn't come up. Finally, Laurie, the younger one, said, "Mary, I think the sun is coming up behind us." And, Mary said, "No, no, the sun comes up over the lake!"

Our early planners like Daniel Burnham, even before Montgomery Ward, recognized that the lake was an important place. He insisted that we preserve this parkland as open land. I think that without Burnham we wouldn't have this Lake Shore Drive. It isn't that the robber barons were the real enemies because you can fight those people. The problem is when people come in for good causes. The La Rabida Sanitarium is a wonderful place, but why did it have to be there? Because it was open land. Why did Mayor Daley want to put the third airport in the lake? Because it was there, open and he didn't have to tear anything down and get anybody mad at him. The problem is that you are resisting against good causes.

If you don't fight every incursion of the lake, pretty soon the lake will be endangered. The closer you get to the lake and the more you can be near the lake, the more valuable it is.

I love Millennium Park and I think that the planners and Mayor Richard M. Daley have done a superb job and I think that they struck the right balance that the public use of that area more than compensates for the fact that they did take some park land, altered some lake views, and some uses of that area are now restricted. But, I think that the off-set in terms of public use is so good that it is worth it.

It is amazing how the Drive is sort of central to all of this because there is such good access to all of these things because of the Drive. I don't like Soldier Field where it is, and I certainly don't like the new version of Soldier Field, but it is so accessible because of the Drive. And, the same is true of McCormick Place, which we fought in the legislature for many, many years. We called that "Tagge's Temple" because George Tagge lobbied so hard for it. I know that it is a source of great revenue for the city and it is one of the attractions of the city, but they used up a lot of parkland and a lot of access to the lake for non-public purposes. I must admit that I am pleasantly surprised at how successful it has been, at least up to now. I don't like the idea, but what made it so attractive in addition to everything else was Lake Shore Drive being there as this wonderful access from the Loop.

I remember the first Democratic Convention that I ever attended in 1952. I was a page or sergeant-at-arms and it was out at the old Stockyard and the route there was so unattractive that Mayor Kennelly had put up facades to cover up the ugly

South Shore Drive from a point 59 feet south of 71st St. (Chicago Historical Society, ICHi-31641, Photographer-J. Sherwin Murphy).

housing as you went out Archer Avenue. That's not true of McCormick Place or Soldier Field because getting there is quite a pleasure.

On the North part of the Drive, all the way from the Edgewater Beach where it swings off the lake to the Loop, there used to be these risers that would rise automatically to control rush hour traffic. It meant that in the morning, when the traffic was coming in, the risers would allow for four lanes going south from the north end and two lanes going north. Then, the risers would go down for most of the day, and, then at night, another riser would rise up on the other side so that you would have four lanes going north and two lanes coming south. It was one of those ideas that sounded so great, because it seemed to be a wonderful way of controlling traffic. However, as the traffic got heavier and heavier, as cars got faster and faster, and as drivers got more and more careless, there were numerous accidents and several fatal accidents because of the risers. Finally, I think that it was under Daley's first term that he took leadership on the idea of the risers and insisted that he get rid of them. That move was very unpopular with the commuters because it did slow up traffic, but it saved a lot of lives,

The other thing about Lake Shore Drive I remember was that the Chicago Tribune had as one of the goals on its masthead the straightening off the Lake Shore Drive "S" curve over the Chicago River. I don't know how it got built that way in the first place, but it was a dangerous stretch of road and slowed up traffic on that part of the Drive. Of all people, the mayor who got rid of the "S" curve was the one that the Tribune never supported—Mayor Harold Washington, who decided that he was going to take that on as one of his issues and did it. The money to do that project came from the failed Crosstown Expressway.

Construction of Oak Street Underpass, July 10, 1964. (Chicago Historical Society, ICHi-34510, Photographer-F. S. Dauwalter).

JIM MCDONOUGH | I started with the city in 1957 and I remember that there was great opposition to Outer Drive East, and I was involved as First Deputy Commissioner of the Department of Streets and Sanitation, and then I became Commissioner in the early 1960s. I was persuaded to take the positions by Mayor Richard J. Daley. He was very nice to me in my career and he used to talk to me at the Morrison and Bismarck Hotels every Monday morning for a half hour to forty-five minutes about the department and streets and sanitation.

As for the "S" curve on the Outer Drive, I wasn't that involved in it because it was more the responsibility of the Department of Planning. We were the lead firm in the work on Lake Shore Drive, and we were the head firm in the reconstruction of lower Wacker Drive, and that leads into the Drive. Over the years we were more involved in maintenance of the Drive while construction was the responsibility of the Department of Public Works under Milton Pikarsky. Our job was to fix the potholes, but we would be involved in traffic engineering because of the fact that street traffic was the responsibility of Streets and Sanitations.

In terms of my own engineering firm, we have done some maintenance kind of work on Lake Shore Drive in some sections, but I don't remember any major work that we have done on the Drive. There was great opposition to straightening out the "S" curve, although I am not certain of the source of the opposition, but I do remember that it was a "hot" item of discussion and very, very sensitive.

WARNER SAUNDERS | They say it was a bone marrow freezing January 30th day in 1935 and the giant white- capped waves had completely closed down Lake Shore Drive at 47th street. Uncle Eddie Northcutt was forced to abandon his plan of using Lake Shore Drive to gather up my mother in his 1941 Plymouth coupe. She had just completed her daily chores at the Epstein's enormous Hyde Park apartment. The night before, my father sent a telegram asking Uncle Eddie to get her to Cook County Hospital as fast as he could.

My dad, a Pullman Porter, was "walking" his way back to Chicago from Miami, hustling between the two assigned sleeping cars of the speeding passenger train. In spite of my mother's delicate condition, Daddy had taken on the extra "run" from another Porter to make a little extra money, because I was on my way into the world, and he knew I would enter naked, hungry and crying!

By the time I was 12 years, I had heard one or more versions of my personal Nativity story from the family about a thousand times especially during Christmas week. That was the year I finally earned $ 25.00, enough money from nearly a whole year of killing and cleaning chickens at Sam and Louie's grocery store to buy a good as new Schwinn "knee action" bicycle on Maxwell Street. But my excitement was tempered by the specter of the long, long, long wait for the snow and ice to give way to dry sidewalks and dreams of riding The Drive. If Easter vacation and a break in the weather lined up at the same time, it was put your Chuck Taylors to the bicycle pedals and the rubber to the road. Finally there would be a chance to leave behind the cold and the unbearable odor blowing east from the Stockyard's killing floors and also from the watchful eyes and heavy hands of the Franciscian nuns. Baby, it was bike riding time! And Lake Shore Drive, here we come!

After all these years, I can still hear Granny Rebecca's words of warning. "You, and Charles, and Bucky be careful after you boys cross Drexel because them white folks don't like you riding your bikes in their neighborhood. Tell them you going swimming in the Lake off 47th street. That's all."

The de-facto "boundaries of "our" neighborhood in those days were roughly Cottage Grove on the east, exactly Wentworth on the west, about 22nd on the north, and "kinda" at 63rd on the south. Thus access to The Lake, depending on its' curve, was five to 15 blocks away from any starting point in our little segregated plot of Chicago called by the white ethnics to the west of us, The Black Belt."

But once we traversed through "enemy territory", that beautiful blue watery heaven was ours for the swimming! We could peddle to 71st on the south and all the way back north to the Edgewater Beach Hotel. The Hyde Park whites, probably great grandparents of the present day lakefront Liberals, weren't at all happy to see us stopping for a dip in God's free water on 57th Street across from the Museum. Those University of Chicago white boys let us know the terms of the 57th Street beach etiquette loudly and clearly, "You little Niggers get the hell off "our" beach. Your "beach" is at 63rd Street. My buddy, Charles, was the smartest boy in our class, but I had the biggest mouth. "This ain't your beach! The Lake belongs to everybody I yelled back at them as we beat a hasty retreat to "our" beach. All along the way, Charles was warning us that our path back was the same as the one going!

Amid all this negativity, along Lake Shore Drive, it was an oasis in the mean spirited and racist urban "desert." The Museum of Science and Industry! The staff who worked there were uncommonly kind and giving. They did all in their power to educate and entertain us. We were encouraged to be hands-on visitors and told to come back frequently, which is what we did. I think they knew we were good kids...boys who came from poor, but good families. We had families who preached education and impressed on us the need to earn our keep in this world.

Those early teachers at the MSI, the Field Museum, the Planetarium, Aquarium, and the Art institute were significant contributors of our early education. Lake Shore Drive was the band of concrete that led us there.

Six years later, as college students home for the summer, Chuck and I would dump the bikes. We used our "political clout" and cajoled then Alderman Ralph Metcalfe to consider us for summer employment. To our pleasant surprise not only did we get jobs together but we were also provided a Park District automobile which was only to be driven back and forth from one end of Lake Shore Drive to the other. Our job? Picking up trash from each of the beaches the old fashion way. A long stick with a large nail at the end was our primary work tool. The big bag slung over our shoulders completed the stylish outfit of the well-dressed "Park District Picker." We used our time wisely by cruising Lake Shore Drive looking for any kind of trash. In addition, we stopped our trash picking and selected a beach here and there, and after taking a dip at those spots, we would have a bite to eat which was usually donated from the generosity of picnicking strangers. And, of course, we also managed to fill our little black phone books with telephone numbers of girls we met along the way.

Over the many years since my youth, there has been a lot of construction and lots of destruction inside of the neighborhoods bordering Lake Shore Drive, but I can't think of one other place in this, my home town, that introduces me to the changing of the seasons like a ride down Lake Shore Drive.

RICHARD DEVINE | The Outer Drive was really tangential to my life because it was just a location, and since we would go to Ardmore Beach we would see the Drive and we were aware of it. Crossing the Drive was quite difficult at times and it was something that you identified with Chicago, just like the Edgewater Beach Hotel and the Nike missile sites. When I began driving, I would go on Lake Shore Drive all the time, and, as a teenager we wouldn't go much further south than downtown. However, when I was playing basketball and football in high school, we would go further south to play schools like St. Rita or Leo. But, it wasn't a situation where you created relationships and would try to visit people on the South Side, although I did have relatives who lived there. Yet, for some reason, my grandmother's place on Thome, between Granville and Devon, was the center point for family get-togethers. So, my relatives would come to visit but I wouldn't go to the South Side to see them at their homes. Thus, Edgewater was the center of my existence and everything was very local in those years, and neighborhoods were the heart of your existence.

POTTER PALMER | I don't have a lot of memories about Lake Shore Drive, except for walking up and down the street when I was a kid. I had friends who lived at 1400, 1420 and 1430 Lake Shore Drive. I do remember taking the Number 51 Sheridan Road double-decker bus for $.05 along Lake Shore Drive to the Saddle and Cycle Club which was located on Foster, just north of the Edgewater Beach Hotel. As I recall, the Outer Drive ended at Foster, and it wasn't until the mid to late 1950s that the Drive was extended to Hollywood Avenue.

In terms of the Gold Coast, there was still a mansion owned by a member of the McCormick family located on the northwest corner of Oak and Michigan that was still there when I was growing up in the neighborhood. Growing up and while going to the Latin School, we used to go to the Esquire Theater for movies and to O'Connell's for hamburgers and cheeseburgers and ice cream almost every Saturday afternoon, but I don't think that we went to the Drake Hotel on a regular basis. If you arrived at O'Connell's about noon there would be nothing but kids from the Latin School and Francis Parker School with their pals getting a table, a hamburger and a Coke, and then going to the movies at the Esquire Theater.

As for other Chicago museums on or close to Lake Shore Drive, there was the Art Institute of Chicago where my great grandmother was one of the original donors of her art collection, and, at one point, my grandfather was the president of the board of the Art Institute. On occasion, we used to also visit the Chicago Historical Society, the Adler Planetarium, the Shedd Aquarium, and, the Field Museum of Natural History.

The only strong recollection I have of a view of the city was from my grandmother and grandfather's apartment at 1301 N. Astor Street during the 1940s (she lived there until she died in 1956). They occupied three floors in this building, the 11th, 12th and 13th floors. I can remember looking south from the window in the living room on the 12th floor, at night, and the biggest thing you could see was the Palmolive Building and the Lindbergh Beacon. The Drake Hotel and the Drake Towers were across the street but were not as prominent. Other than that, nothing blocked our view of the lake and downtown. The 1300 N. Lake Shore Drive block had no buildings and just an open field. Once in a while, we joined other kids on that block in pick-up baseball games.

Lincoln Park had three meanings for me. When I was young, my mother arranged for my sister and me to have horseback riding lessons. So we would go over to a stable near Lincoln Park West. We would ride our horses on city streets to North Avenue and Clark Street where there was a bridle path in Lincoln Park.

I also attended the Boys Latin School located on North Dearborn Parkway just south of North Avenue (there was also a separate Girls Latin School in those years). At recess, or in the afternoon, after class, we would go to Lincoln Park where we would play games, including "kick the can" at the Grant's Tomb Monument. My third recollection is that on Sunday mornings my sister and I would be sent to Sunday School at St. Christendom's. My mother (who never went to church) would send us there. Following that, we would walk into Lincoln Park and go to the zoo in the morning, and, depending on the weather, we would look at the animals inside the various buildings or outside in their cages or enclosures. Then, we would all have lunch at my grandmother's apartment. (This was before the National Football League so that people weren't glued to their television sets all Sunday afternoons). Then, in the afternoon, we might go to the Chicago Historical Society where they had Sunday afternoon movies in their auditorium.

I lived in that area until I was in my early 20s and finally lived at 1301 N. Astor like my grandparents. My pals from kindergarten through 7th grade, before I went to an East Coast prep school, were from Latin School. So, every day, when I was old enough, I would ride my bike on the city streets to school...when I was younger I would be walked there by my nurse. I knew the whole area, and when I was older, my pals and I would have dinner at our various apartments and then we would meet at about 8 pm during the summer months and just walk around the neighborhood. We knew a lot of other kids from school, and although the parents weren't too happy about it, we would drop in on friends' apartments or at their houses in the neighborhood. We would ring the door bell, and if we were invited in, we would go in and have a little party. We all knew every nook, cranny and alley throughout the neighborhood stretching from Oak Street up to North Avenue, and in the winter, we used to go sledding when the snow would cover the overpass that led to North Avenue Beach.

TOM O'GORMAN | It is interesting that Lake Shore Drive was built in increments and it was really when Kelly was Chicago's mayor and Kennelly was a Chicago businessman that the last major part of Outer Drive was completed. And, if you go to Madonna de la Strada Chapel at Loyola University and you go to what you would call the front door to the church and open those doors (the name Madonna de la Strada means Our Lady of the Highway/Streets) it opens into Sheridan Road because that was what Lake Shore Drive was supposed to become. The Drive was supposed to run along the lake to there but that was the segment of the Drive that was never completed. So, where all those apartment buildings are located from 5800 Sheridan Road all the way up to Evanston that was originally supposed to be the highway.

The Marshall Field family donated all of the bridle paths along Lake Michigan to the City of Chicago, and today those are running paths. Dorsey Connors, the journalist whose father was the State Senator from the 42nd Ward, and whose "Dutch" uncle was Dorsey Crowe, the alderman of that ward, told me that people used to be able to ride their horses from downtown to the Saddle and Cycle Club and there were stables along the park. Dorsey used to do that all the time.

In 1937, President Franklin Roosevelt came to Chicago to open the final part of the bridge over the Chicago River on the "S" curve. I always remember the story that Roosevelt came as a personal favor to Cardinal Mundelein, but, in return, Mundelein's payment to Roosevelt was that he would not stand in the way of Felix Frankfurter's appointment to the U.S. Supreme Court. Roosevelt came to Mundelein's house and he had lunch with him there before dedicating the bridge. The entrance to the city's harbor at the river changed quite often over the years, and it had a variety of lives including when it really was redone and the engineer who oversaw all of that for the U.S. Army Corps of Engineers was Captain Jefferson Davis, later the President of the Confederacy.

FR.DAVID DILLION, CARMELITE PRIEST, FORMER PRINCIPAL/PRESIDENT OF MT CARMEL HIGH SCHOOL |

My family joined South Shore Country Club back when I was in the fifth grade in 1950, and it became a wonderful place to go for Sunday evening dinner. I remember John, the doorman, who would open the door and we would go into the main building of the club. We would walk down the long corridor or promenade and it would lead to a beautiful Dining room. After dinner, there would be a Sunday evening movie in the ballroom. This was before television played such a prominent role in our lives, and it was long before the Internet. So, to go there and enjoy the Sunday evening dinner and Sunday evening movie was just a wonderful way to end one week and begin the next.

It was a private club. It was originally started, probably without any or very few Catholic members in 1905, by the majority Protestant community in South Shore. As the years went by, more and more Catholics became more affluent and joined the Country Club, and they became a majority in the Club. That, of course, was before the Civil Rights Movement initiated by Martin Luther King in 1964.

Aerial view of South Lake Shore Drive,
including Meigs Field, Field Museum,
Soldier Field and McCormick Place, c. 1990.
(Courtesy of The Walsh Group)

In the 1950's there was no black community in South Shore and no black members of the club. It was just not thought of back in those days. Thanks be to God, we've come a long way since then.

Growing up in Our Lady of Peace Parish at 79th and Jeffrey, and living at 76th and Constance, when we were about 12 years old and in 7th grade, in the summer time, a group of us would get on the 75th street bus for a two mile ride east to the 75th street beach, called Rainbow Beach. I have so many memories of playing on the beach and in Lake Michigan. Then the opportunity came along to go to the beach at the South Shore Country Club. It was a very nice and pleasant beach as well, and I met new friends there. There was also a smaller dining room just adjacent to the beach called the Bird Cage, a great place for lunch or a snack. Also, I was introduced to horseback riding at the Country club. I could go to the club every Saturday and take horseback riding lessons, which was a new and interesting experience. Needless to say, I would not have had the opportunity to ride a horse elsewhere and it was a very nice thing about being a member of the country club. In addition to the horseback riding, every year the club would also have a riding show and as children, we would all be in that contest, and our parents would be watching and encouraging us from the "sidelines." It was a social event and all part of growing up and just a great thing about the South Side and the lakefront.

In addition, there were tennis courts at the club, although I was not a tennis player myself. The tennis courts were very comfortable and it was a nice amenity. In addition, there was a small, nine-hole golf course, and people would play 18 holes by going around a second time. Many of my friends were caddies at the golf course. The Country club offered so many amenities with the restaurants, the Sunday evening movies, swimming in the summertime, the older folks playing golf, those who played tennis, and there were also many social events in the Ballroom.

In September of 1957, I entered the Seminary in my first year of college, so I didn't personally get involved in a lot of the social events at the club. But, as a younger person, I can recall my parents going to the Christmas ball and other parties during the year, and they had a wonderful Easter brunch there every year. The South Shore Country Club, now the South Shore Cultural Center, is east of Lake Shore Drive and its entire western boundary is South Shore Drive, from 67th to 72nd Streets.

Growing up in South Shore so many experiences of driving down Lake Shore Drive come to mind. We would leave our home at 76th street; get on Jeffrey

Boulevard and drive north to get on the Drive at 67th and start downtown. It was always such a beautiful drive and I thoroughly enjoyed it. When I was 15, I did have a job working at my dad's company as an office boy one summer. And, again, going to work every day and going down Lake Shore Drive was a wonderful way to start the day and a wonderful way to end the day with the beauty of the lakefront.

I came back to Mt. Carmel High School in 1967 as a Carmelite priest and teacher. Mt. Carmel is located at 6410 Dante Avenue. So many times I would go over to Lake Shore Drive and jog along the Drive or bike along the Drive because it was such a beautiful place. One of the great things about Chicago is that the lakefront belongs to the people. In most other cities, buildings go right down to the waterfront. But, in Chicago, thanks be to God, the lakefront is all public property from 7200 South up to 5800 North. It all belongs to the people. We are so blessed to have the Outer Drive and have it as part of our lives. And, thanks be to God, private development was never allowed on Lake Shore Drive along that public park area going back to 1893 when the land was all filled in for Jackson Park. It was all marshland, and it was developed for the World's Fair of 1893. Eventually it became Jackson Park and helped make Lake Shore Drive such a beautiful place to drive on.

Most of the memories I reflect on are South Side memories. People naturally identify themselves with their community. One of the interesting things in Chicago, especially on the South Side, is that many people identify themselves by their parish community. In South Shore we came from Our Lady of Peace Parish while others in South Shore came from St. Phillip Nieri or St. Brides. We are all South Siders and we are proud of our South Side roots.

BILL ZWECKER | I have been all over the world and I can say that I have never seen a more beautiful urban roadway. I would say that because of its proximity to the lake and the parks along the whole stretch of it, and even the residential high rises, make this interesting wall that goes down to the Drive—and then you have the water. The lake is a huge part of it. The only place that would come close to Lake Shore Drive might be places that people talk about like the Champs Elysees (which is certainly wonderful, charming and impressive). But, I still maintain that Lake Shore Drive is the most beautiful urban roadway. There are a lot of major international cities like London (the Mall), Paris (the Champs Elysees), and Buenos Aires that have big, wide streets, similar to Michigan Avenue. But, there is something about the combination of architecture and water and the natural beauty and the trees in the parks that all come together to give it a very unique urban transportation setting.

My connection to Lake Shore Drive literally started at birth because my mother went into labor when we lived on Melrose and I was born at Passavant Hospital which became part of Northwestern University Hospital. My mother, the late Peg Zwecker, always told the story about my father driving her down Lake Shore Drive on Christmas Eve as she went into labor. At that time, what was then the Palmolive Building used to have a lighted cross during the holidays on the top of the building. So, mom was looking up at that, it was Christmas Eve, she was in labor, and she knew that she was going to deliver on Christmas Day. Of course, that story was recounted to me from the time I could understand things said to me.

My mother worked for the *Chicago Daily News*, and when I was born, she was with the *Chicago Sun-Times*, and then she went back to the *Daily News* in 1950, and my dad always worked downtown. So, we would come down to the Loop often, and they would always want to take me over to Grant Park. One of my earliest memories, frankly, of Lake Shore Drive was going to the Lincoln Park Zoo, which I loved, because I had an aunt who lived on Lincoln Park West that overlooked the Zoo. We would go over there and we could see the Drive, and

I remember all of that. I also remember going on the Drive to Hyde Park because I had a godmother who lived there and we would go see her. I just always remember that Lake Shore Drive was so cool, and it was right next to the lake. Of course I remember when they made all the changes to the Museum Campus.

I lived on Lake Shore Drive as an adult. My first apartment, when I came back to Chicago after I had graduated from college and had worked for Senator Chuck Percy in Washington, DC for about a year, was in apartment 1407 at 1360 N. Lake Shore Drive. The interesting thing was that was on the site of the old Potter Palmer estate, close to the corner of Schiller and the Drive, on the south side of Schiller and the north side of Banks. The apartment building was erected on the site when they tore down the old mansion and was managed by Draper and Kramer. That was my first apartment on my own back in the city, and I always remember that the selling point for living there was that every apartment had a view of the lake. I was in a one-bedroom apartment that was pretty far set back, but you could go to the windows in the living room and see the lake.

Then, I got married, and we lived on Lakeview before moving to the suburbs. After a divorce I moved back and lived at 3270 N. Lake Shore Drive, which was a building owned by the Wirtz family. The story was that Arthur Wirtz reportedly picked up the entire block during the Depression for $90,000 because everybody was bankrupt. It overlooked Belmont Harbor, and I lived there for three to four years. It was a great building and it was a rental apartment. The only other place where I lived directly on Lake Shore Drive was 3750 N. Lake Shore Drive, a co-op building, and I also lived at 257 East Delaware, which is just a half block from the Drive, long before that.

As a kid, one memory I have of Lake Shore Drive was when my dad was a member of the old Lake Shore Club and that was where I learned how to swim. And, I remember this bratty kid, whose father was kind of important although I didn't know who he was at the time, who was not very nice to me in the pool...it was Rich Daley. I have kidded Bill Daley and Michael Daley, but not the mayor about this, because when the three of them were in the pool they were hellions.

The museums meant a lot to me. My father and mother were involved in the Art Institute and it amazes me that after all these years and times going to that museum that there is so much at the Art Institute that I haven't seen. I realize that you will never see it all. As for the other museums, I loved going to the Field Museum and looking at all the specimens and I was more interested in the Shedd Aquarium than the Adler Planetarium over the years. When I was a lot younger I used to play on softball teams at Grant Park, near the Drive.

I do remember going to the Edgewater Beach Hotel with my folks for special occasions. I remember once being up there because for some reason there was an event at the hotel and I have a photo with my mother and dad and John and Eunice Johnson. That would have been in the late '50s or early '60s.

I remember driving up and down Lake Shore Drive because my sister went to Northwestern University in Evanston and my friends had a lot of friends in Evanston. I recall going to South Shore Country Club when my godmother's daughter had her marriage reception there in the mid-1950s. So, when we would drive along Lake Shore Drive it felt like being on the ocean. I always loved the blue top to the Furniture Mart at 680 N. Lake Shore Drive and then the one on the South Michigan building near the Stevens Hotel.

The city and the Drive have evolved in a good way, and as things change the concept of "forever open, free and clear" is still being followed. Another Lake Shore Drive memory is Meigs Field which is Northerly Island. I had an uncle who had a tiny Piper Cub airplane and he used to fly into Meigs Field and I remember how cool it was to land there with the whole city in a spectacular way in front of the little airport.

When Mayor Daley did his "midnight conversion" of Meigs Field, the very next weekend I was in Los Angeles for a press conference for a Harrison Ford movie and I was just doing a television interview with him. He knew that I was from Chicago, and he said, "Chicago! You tell that Mayor Daley I am so pissed at him for what he did to that airport!"

RICHARD WARD | The New East Side, historically, had Lake Shore Drive running through it and originally was right between the Buckingham and the Outer Drive East. It was the notorious "S" curve as referred to in old pictures with two ninety degree turns. It was lined up with the lakefront as it went by Grant Park, then it went between Outer Drive East and the Buckingham, and then made a 90 degree turn to the east and then another 90 degree turn back to the north and went across the Lake Shore Drive bridge over the Chicago River. That bridge had been completed in 1937 and was dedicated by President Franklin Delano Roosevelt that year.

When they built the Lake Shore Drive Bridge it had a second level. That second level was originally designed to be for railroads because this was a railroad yard and it was the way to get to the other side of the river. Ultimately, that was never used for railroads and it became lower Lake Shore Drive Bridge. At one point, there was going to be an interchange that was going to go along the river, but that never happened. Outer Drive East was built here in 1961. In 1973, Harbor Point was built and when there were only those two buildings here they realigned Lake Shore Drive to get rid of that notorious "S" curve that was a very high accident area. They realigned it in 1985-1986.

NEIL HARTIGAN | I suppose that my first experience with Lake Shore Drive, other than riding on it all sorts of different ways when I was young was that I swam in the lake all the time. The portion of the Drive from Foster north to Hollywood didn't exist at the time I was growing up in Roger Park and in grammar school. The Edgewater Beach Hotel, which was one of the most famous grand hotels of America, with its boardwalk was extremely well known both for water sports and a place that had a real history in terms of music. My uncle, Frank "Tweet" Hogan, who lived next door to us, had a great band, and he played at the Edgewater Beach. The hotel had the famed Marine Room and great Hollywood entertainers who performed there. So, I was there on a variety of different occasions. In addition, I swam there because we had friends who lived in the Edgewater Beach Apartments. Or I would be at the hotel at a party, and we would wade into the lake off the beach. That whole area of water and beach became an important part of the Outer Drive.

As far as I know, I don't think that there was any organized opposition to the decision to extend the Drive from Foster to Bryn Mawr and then to Hollywood, but I don't know the reasons for building the highway around the Edgewater Beach Hotel. One of the issues was that the traffic when it came off the Drive at Foster was almost impossible and it became very difficult for that kind of a hotel there to function. So I would imagine that the extension, at least in part, was a way to reduce congestion.

From Hollywood northward, the developers were buying the houses and the mansions and then knocking them down and beginning to build along the stretch to Devon, and they weren't doing anything about the roadway. So, the volume of people coming out of those buildings onto a two-way street was an ongoing mess.

As for my family's interest in stopping the expansion of the Drive from Hollywood all the way to Evanston, the first time would have been my dad's efforts. In those days, the 49th Ward went south to Bryn Mawr and I think that he was involved in that effort. When dad ran for alderman he was the City Treasurer.

It would have been 1954-1955. He was very publicly outspoken about stopping the stealing of the beaches and the destruction of the lakefront by the developers who were knocking down the houses and putting up the high rises with the resulting population density. He said that if he were elected alderman that it would never happen again, and it never did. The fact that there is only one new high rise building in the ward, and it wasn't on the lakefront but on Loyola University's campus, is testament to my father. It also says that the idea against further high rises was right, and it is still right.

In the late 1960s through the early 1980s, Loyola University was in favor of extending the Drive to Evanston. While we were living in Rogers Park in St. Ignatius Parish, and during the time I was Lieutenant Governor of Illinois, I became involved in issues related to the lakefront.

I certainly was always opposed to the extension of Lake Shore Drive from Hollywood to Evanston. What is the point of the extension anyway? It would be one thing if you were just extending the Drive from Hollywood to Devon. But if you are going to then destroy all of East Rogers Park, you would have to build a concrete wall and "kill" the street end beaches which would have to be moved east of the highway. It would lead to the end of beaches and

parks like Hartigan Park, North Shore Beach, Pratt, and Columbia that are located at the ends of residential streets that are enhanced by having recreation opportunities.

Also, apartment density is not the most attractive thing for young families in houses. The question was how could we keep the Rogers Park neighborhood alive when everybody was moving to the Northwest Side and the North and Northwest suburbs? We worked for public safety, good education, public transportation and recreation in the neighborhoods. Even with that, it was tough until the condominiums came in, and then we had more stability. But, those are all important elements and if you look at the regeneration that is going on in Rogers Park right now, they clearly are. I thought that the extension of the Drive was a bad idea, and I still think it is and would oppose such a development.

When I was the Chicago Park District attorney, I bought all the open space that I could find on the lakefront—every place. We did land banking, so that anything that was vacant I bought, up and down the entire Drive. In fact, that's the way the Broadway Armory became the Broadway Park. I did that too when I was Lieutenant Governor. But, for instance, if you look at Lane Park located on Thorndale and the lake, it was nothing, and look at it now. And, at Granville,

which is now Berger Park, the developer actually put a steel retaining wall in the lake. Well, the idea was to give him more square footage. He was saying that half the street was his because he had bought up the property on the street. And, therefore the retaining wall was appropriate. I went to court myself, which I didn't often do, and got the retaining wall physically pulled back out.

Then, we created Berger Park in the parkway. The developers still had the property, but the city's part was the parkway. We named it after Miles Berger who had grown up in Edgewater and his dad had been very active in real estate there. I got Esther Saperstein, the State Senator, to put in the bill in Springfield to buy the Viatorian's property. Then the Park District was able to condemn it and that was how Berger Park happened. We not only took the retaining wall out, but we redid that beach and did the same thing at Devon. Albion Beach was there, and we took all the street ends in Rogers Park and called a landscape expert in and created the beaches. If you go to the end of North Shore Avenue, you can walk on sand from Albion to the northern end of the city. It was all part of an ongoing effort to enhance the livability and protect the environment. So, it became a case for sustainable development.

Let's say, hypothetically, that Lake Shore Drive gets extended up to Devon.

Aerial view of South Lake Shore Drive,
looking towards the Museum of Science
and Industry and Hyde Park, c. 1990.
(Courtesy of The Walsh Group)

But then the question becomes where does it go from Devon? You can go west and widen Devon, but, if you are going to swing north, you have a major congestion problem on Sheridan Road to Evanston. The bottle neck going into Evanston would be a real problem at Calgary Cemetery. So, let's say you extended Lake Shore Drive to Howard Street. What does that accomplish? All that does is to destroy the current beaches.

If you are going to do it correctly then you are going to have to take the Drive all the way along into Evanston, Wilmette, and all the way up the North Shore. The fights you would have opposing this idea in Evanston and all the way up the North Shore would be enormous. Can you imagine their beaches being taken to build the extension of the Drive?

JUDGE MARVIN ASPEN | My earliest memories as a child of Lake Shore Drive are driving to the beach in the family car with my parents, pre-air conditioning, on a very hot, muggy summer night. We parked somewhere between Foster and Montrose, walked to the grass, and lay down on a blanket to enjoy the cool, summer air before returning to our hot, stuffy apartment in Albany Park. We didn't sleep there all night, but we did spend a good part of the evening there. This was probably my first real memory of doing something as a family, because it was such a change in our regular routine. Other early memories are of driving on Lake Shore Drive, going to the museums, the Field Museum, the Aquarium and Planetarium, and the Museum of Science and Industry, which we used to call the Rosenwald Museum.

My recollection of the Lake Shore Drive in those early years was soon supplemented by the tremendous building boom post World War II, along the Drive. I can recall driving down Lake Shore Drive, seeing the beautiful expanse which was a great contrast to the homes and the apartment buildings in Albany Park and the fact that the difference in density was significant. The experience was probably similar to a drive into the country by a poorer urban family. I can't think of any urban American area that I have seen, and I think that I have been to quite a few of them, where there is anything as beautiful as Lake Shore Drive. Even the urban drive around San Francisco near the ocean and city to me does not compare with Lake Shore Drive. The Drive is beautiful because of the contrasting vistas of the parks, the beach, the buildings and the skyline. Driving from the north, going south, you see green in the summertime and snow in the wintertime, and the Lake mostly calm, but sometimes blustery and as spectacular

Aerial view of South Lake Shore Drive
construction east of the Museum of Science
and Industry, c. 1990.
(Courtesy of The Walsh Group)

as any ocean because of its immensity. On your east is the beauty of the grass and the sand and the lake, and to the west, the architecture of the buildings. But, if you look straight ahead, you see the skyline of the city emerge as you move along the Drive. We take this beautiful vista for granted, but when you have visitors come to the city and you take them on that same trip for their first time, you can have a new appreciation through their eyes for what a spectacular vista it is.

To me, the trip away from the city going north on the Drive is never quite as spectacular. You have your back to the city. And, when you drive into the biggest urban-planning mistake that the city has made, the horror of the stretch on Sheridan Road, where the Drive ends at Hollywood and goes north into Sheridan. Sheridan Road is a canyon of apartment buildings on both sides from Hollywood through Devon. To me, that was the greatest disaster in planning that was questionably pushed through the City Council. Better planning would have had the Drive go all the way to Evanston, which might have been a fairly easy thing to do at the time.

So, as good an example of urban planning as Lake Shore Drive has been, as bad an example of urban planning is that unattractive stretch on Sheridan Road from Hollywood to Devon. I don't think realistically that we will ever be able to expand Lake Shore Drive north from Hollywood. Sheridan Road is relatively narrow, and, you have apartment buildings and other structures very close to the road. In today's economy it would also be a pipe dream to hope to reverse this planning disaster.

The Drive and the lakefront have always been a special part of my life. I was the judge in a case when Loyola University attempted to build out into the lake. I ruled that they could not do so because, by law, the Lake belongs to the public and, in effect, a private group, even a non-profit institution like Loyola could not usurp the lakebed for its own purposes.

I was also the judge in another case won by the Friends of the Parks cancelling the erection of new entry ramps on Lake Shore Drive. In that case, city traffic engineers had wanted to make extensive changes in the ramp systems at Belmont and Fullerton. It would have involved them taking some Park District land and for new concrete structures. This would have changed the look of the Lakefront, and, more importantly, it would have usurped public parkland, to both widen and lengthen both entrance and exit ramps.

Every time I drive down Edens or I-94, and see those big semi trucks, or you visit other cities like Cleveland and see those same trucks with their noise, bulk, and added congestion driving along the city lakefront, I know how fortunate we are in Chicago. So, whatever you call Lake Shore Drive, it is truly an urban drive as opposed to a commercial throughway with all the congestion and noise and lack of beauty that comes with an interstate highway.

In essence, the dream of Burnham, Olmsted and other city planners has come true on the city's lakefront. You can go to Pittsburgh, Cleveland or Milwaukee and you can take the same drive along the road closest to the lake, and not only is the vista different but your companion vehicles sharing the road are significantly different.

I remember also the great snowstorm of 1967 and how it closed Lake Shore Drive. To my knowledge, that is the only time that the Drive was closed for a snowstorm. As I recall, the Drive was closed for at least four or five days after the storm. Cars were buried there and you could walk up and down the Drive and the snow was practically over your head. When I remember the sight from the perspective of our apartment windows on the 14th floor of 4950 Marine Drive, it was surreal to see the whole Drive covered over with several feet of snow and only the roofs of the cars visible.

ERMA TRANTER, PRESIDENT, FRIENDS OF THE PARKS | I remember my first impression of Lake Shore Drive vividly. I was born and raised in the Detroit, in the city. My parents were immigrants from Italy, so we never really travelled and my father died when I was young, and I had never been to Chicago. My late husband had a job opportunity here, and I decided to give up teaching and go to graduate school. So, we drove from Detroit and we first went through Gary. It had smoke-filled air in billowing clouds, and there was a smell when you came through that city, so strong that I remember rolling up the car windows. When we went through Gary, I was a little concerned about it. I was thinking steel mills, and where am I going, since Chicago is just a little further north of Gary and was this experience I was going to have in Chicago. But, when we got onto Lake Shore Drive and its park system, I just thought the city was beautiful, and I loved my exposure to Lake Michigan for the first time.

I think that it was early afternoon when we arrived in the city, and the quality of light in the city was stunning. My first impression was that Chicago was a beautiful city. I had never experienced such a lakefront before, especially coming from Detroit with its Eight Mile Road. So, I was very happy here, and I felt from the very beginning that this was an exciting, livable city and I still feel that way today.

Chicago has just become more beautiful and our lakefront certainly is one of the key components that make this city so great.

In my many travels, I have never seen an urban roadway as attractive as Lake Shore Drive. The roadway itself has gotten more beautiful and Friends of the Parks had a hand in that. In the 1980s, the lake was beautiful, but, at that time, the road had New Jersey barriers in some parts of it to separate north and southbound traffic. We forget the work that has been done since the 1980s to absolutely beautify the Drive. Prior to that, the lakefront was beautiful but Lake Shore Drive wasn't particularly planted or as green as it is today. But, in the 1980s, (Friends of the Parks was formed in 1975), there was a plan by CDOT/IDOT with federal money to expand ramps at Fullerton and Belmont. They did data collecting and they found that there were higher incidents of accidents at those two ramps (the entrance ramp at Fullerton and the exit ramp at Belmont). They said that they were too short and didn't give cars enough time to blend into the traffic. They had a proposal to widen all four ramps, even though two of the ramps didn't have any higher accident rates, but they were geometrically balancing it out. And, they were taking these ramps and widening them into Lincoln Park on both sides at highway standards.

So, they were using the expressway standard of 55 mph which meant that you were making them really long and you were making them really wide. And, this was Lake Shore Drive as a boulevard. It had been designed as a boulevard and it actually evolved historically as just a carriage road. Some suggested that it was Potter Palmer who wanted to increase the value of his lakefront property who wanted this carriage route. So, it started as a carriage route, became a boulevard, and when Friends of the Parks reviewed the plan it was apparent that engineers were unnecessarily beginning to use highway standards on the boulevard and they were converting excessive parkland into highway.

We have only filed two lawsuits in our 35 years and this was one of them. Since there were federal dollars involved for the roadway, the suit went to Federal Court, which was a good thing. We won that suit and U.S. District Court Judge Marvin Aspen reiterated that Lake Shore Drive was a boulevard and that they would have to redesign those ramps into boulevard standards. That was the start of it. Then, because of that lawsuit and the judge's decision, it served to recognize the Friends of the Parks as a non-profit concerned about the aesthetics of the park system and its role in protecting the park system and the Drive as a result.

Aerial view of South Lake Shore Drive
and Illinois Central Railroad tracks, c. 1990.
(Courtesy of The Walsh Group)

A couple of years later, in the later 1980s, CDOT said that they had to fix something on Lake Shore Drive because there had been crossover accidents and several people had been killed. One of the newspapers was making a major thrust on this issue. They said that we have to protect those lives, and we were in complete agreement with that position.

Then, CDOT came in and said to us, "You have a choice. Would you (Friends of the Parks) prefer a New Jersey barrier (those concrete barriers that you put all along a highway). Or would you prefer one of those steel railings that are used on the highway." At the time, those were the only two solutions that CDOT could think of to put between them. We said, this is a boulevard and the Federal Court has issued a statement saying that Lake Shore Drive is a boulevard, but CDOT is still coming up with two standards that apply to highways, both the New Jersey barrier and the metal guardrail.

We said to CDOT, "Let us work together, do some research on national parks, like those in Colorado, Utah and California, to discover what they do, because we know that, in many cases, they wouldn't use this solution in national parks." To CDOT's credit, they told us that they would do some research.

At the time, Walter Netsch was the president of the Board of the Chicago Park District, and being from Skidmore, Owings and Merrill, and a well known architect, he was amenable to working with us and using his visual, architectural background to helping come up with a solution. The solution was what I think made Lake Shore Drive more beautiful...where it wasn't, I think it is now. It's a pleasure because there are trees, it's green, it's flowered, and it is planted. In the late '80s, there were many design and community meetings that included our group and Walter, and we came up with the concept of planting trees in a median in Lake Shore Drive.

The built median would be a concrete planter, not a New Jersey barrier. The idea was for it to be a designed, concrete wall on both sides and filled with soil and planted with trees. Interestingly, in the late '80s, the highway engineers who, in earlier decades had never thought about aesthetics were now coming to understand that aesthetics played a role. They supported the design that you now see on North Lake Shore Drive. It started on that part of the Drive because that was where most of the crossover accidents were occurring. The median dividers were constructed in 1989 and then came the plantings, and have become a feature that we all agree has improved the aesthetics of the Drive.

Mayor Harold Washington was in office at the time the work was being designed, but even Mayor Richard M. Daley promotes trees and has been very supportive of the beautified North Lake Shore Drive. And, anytime there has been any further expansion there was always a landscape plan that was detailed and implemented.

In addition, as Mayor Daley said, in the winter when they salt the roads, it can do damage to the plants. One of the things that the city did was drop the speed limit on Lake Shore Drive to 40 mph to reduce the splashing and salt damage to the trees. They also put up some fabric over the plantings to provide further protection. We know Chicago has a harsh environment, but the trees seem to be doing fairly well.

It takes a long time to get roadway plans and funding takes years, and finally things get constructed, and they do it in segments. As for the South Side, Friends of the Parks wanted to know how we could do something on that part of Lake Shore Drive, so we worked on that during the 1990s and there was a major improvement of the Drive which was tremendous in terms of citizen advocacy. Then, beyond that, we wrote to CDOT and IDOT and asked them to start looking for funds for the south lakefront because they should have equal change and beautification of Lake Shore Drive. At that time they had those metal crash barriers in between and they hadn't done as much planting. It took us several years to keep on pushing them to try to find the funding. In the end, they did find the funding and they are redoing South Lake Shore Drive, and they included citizen participation in that process.

Because we had been party to that one lawsuit, they very much wanted our support and that helped us to have a role in the redesign of South Lake Shore Drive similar to North Lake Shore Drive. So, the community met many times with Alderman Toni Preckwinkle, and a similar concept to the North Drive was created and they even tweaked the concrete a little bit in terms of design. In the end, there were plantings, and where they had wide median dividers, they did more plantings.

If you just go south of 23rd Street there is a very large space between the north and south bound lanes and parts of it are narrow, but it is a decorative barrier that has been safety tested and approved. It also accomplished what CDOT was trying to accomplish to prevent serious cross-over accidents, but it was done in an aesthetically pleasing way. It goes all the way south through Jackson Park, and the last area they did was around 66th and Marquette Road.

They did some grade underpasses there and when they did the underpasses they were restored at those locations. The design of the bridges and the design of the underpasses and the design of the planted median dividers are harmonious and beautiful. The next phase will be at the former United States Steel plant. The entire experience of being on Lake Shore Drive, if you are in a car, is extraordinarily improved, overall.

My experience with working with the traffic engineers since the early 1980s is that they are only concerned about one thing, and that is moving traffic. So, we had some struggles with highway engineers when they were doing work in parks. I think our history shows that prior to the 1980s we had some problems with our parks. If you look early on before our organization was even formed, what they did in Jackson Park was that there was a fight about building a highway through that park. Some of the roads that they did ultimately build have been harmful because there weren't as many environmentalists and park activists. So, you have Cornell, which is really wide and is kind of a highway kind of road cutting through Jackson Park. You have Garfield Boulevard at 55th going through Washington Park, and that is one we all want to change, take back and make it more park-like. But, it is like eight lanes through Washington Park, an historic

Olmsted design park. In some places, it is like twelve lanes and confusing to use in spots. Who were these traffic engineers who created this in the 1960s? So, you look at some of our parks and some of the roadways that were put through them and it is kind of tragic.

The 1980s was a tremendous change because they were willing...and I do think that the lawsuit really was an impetus for this...to reaffirm that Lake Shore Drive was a boulevard. By the '80s they were saying, "We will step back and take some time and work with you and the citizens to come up with a better design."

I think that this is not just a Chicago thing, but in the 1980s environmental issues were beginning to take root in other cities. We are seeing that if you beautify something, everyone wants to be there. When things look good, it is a gathering space. So, there was a new concept of city design in the '80s taking root totally different than in the '60s which are malls, roadways and cars. Now there is new thinking. So, you get San Francisco that had built the high roadway along the Embarcadero, an elevated roadway that blocked off their greatest treasure which was their waterfront. But, by the 1980s, they were recognizing that and they demolished that and took down an entire expressway. That happened in Boston with the superstructures up against the Atlantic Ocean and their water-front, their natural resource. It took them billions of dollars to do the "Big Dig," and they dug it underground, recognizing that they wanted economic development, jobs, property values, and tourists. They decided that it couldn't be accomplished with multiple levels of a highway in the air blocking views to their waterfront. They bit the bullet, got a lot of federal funding and removed that highway and put it underground.

MARC SCHULMAN | To me the heart of Lake Shore Drive, ground zero, would be the corner of Oak Street and Michigan Avenue. My father opened his first restaurant in that area, Eli's Stage Delicatessen, on Oak near Rush in 1962, when I was seven years old. I certainly remember trick or treating on Oak Street, the Kennedy Assassination in 1963, and my bar mitzvah in 1966 when *Born Free* was playing at the Esquire Theater. When we moved to that community they were building 1000 Lake Shore Drive Plaza and my father's dear friend, Ira Colitz, lived in the penthouse there. He was a politician who was related to Harold Pearlman, who built the building. I should add that for most of my life, other than when I attended high school in the suburbs, I lived within a few blocks of Lake Shore Drive.

At the time I was born my family lived at 5757 N. Sheridan Road at Balmoral, a block from the end of Lake Shore Drive and near the Edgewater Beach Hotel. The road has always been very important to me. But, it was really Oak Street that brought my family to the Near North Side in 1962 when we opened our first restaurant in that area. Then in 1966, dad opened Eli's, The Place for Steak. And, in 1968, we had to close the deli when we had a fire there. When I graduated from high school, in 1972, we lived at 990 N. Lake Shore Drive just after it was built.

So, after we moved there, other than going to college, I have always lived within a couple of blocks of the Drive. I attended Northwestern University Law School and went to school, literally, on Lake Shore Drive, and I used to play football at Lake Shore Park. Then, after my father died, Seneca Park and Eli Schulman Playground were dedicated to him. So, I think that while Lake Shore Drive is certainly a highway to get to places, it is something pretty spectacular looking out over the lake from Lake Shore Drive and driving down a highway so significant and unique to Chicago. To me, when you try to explain Chicago to someone, it is a city that ends at a lakefront that is open, free and protected by a roadway from one end of the city to the other.

CHAPTER 5
COMPLETING LAKE SHORE DRIVE
1987–2004

1996
Last major reconfiguration of Lake Shore
Drive is completed with south and northbound
traffic flowing west of Soldier Field.
New parkland and secondary park roads are
constructed as part of new Museum Campus
where northbound Drive lanes were
previously located.

1996
Museum Campus opens.

2003
Rebuilt Soldier Field, with capacity of
61,500, opens on September 29.

2004
Millennium Park completed, turning
Grant Park into one of city's top two tourist
attractions. Navy Pier is the other.

Millennium Park, 2005.
(Courtesy of The Walsh Group).

DAN WALSH AND DALE SWANBERG | *Daniel J. Walsh and Dale Swanberg of The Walsh Group discuss the construction company's key involvement in the modernization of Lake Shore Drive and many of the buildings and museums that adjoin it. Here is an edited version of their remarks:*

Swanberg: The only major job that The Walsh Group didn't do on the Drive since the mid 1990s was straightening of the "S" Curve. In combination with the straightening of the "S" Curve was replacing the movable bascule bridge over the river. Every linear foot of pavement south of the bridge down to La Rabida in Jackson Park, we have rebuilt. We built the Museum Campus including all the parks, the lakefront restoration around the Adler Planetarium and the Shedd Aquarium.

Walsh: We did all the greenscapes from the water to the Outer Drive throughout the Museum Campus. We renovated the second McCormick Place about 15 years ago, including the Arie Crown Theater and the two exhibition halls. As for the Museum Campus, we have done several projects there, including the Field Museum, and we have just done the complete renovation of the Shedd Aquarium.

Swanberg: We moved Lake Shore Drive from the east side of Soldier Field to the west side in 1996. And, in 1997 and into 1998, we built the Museum Campus.

Walsh: As for Soldier Field, about 25 years ago, we rebuilt the concrete stands inside the stadium because they were falling down. The Park District had put a sand load test on the stands right before the 50 yard line before the coming season and they just fell down. So, we went in there and rebuilt them. All the stands, from goal post to goal post, on the west and east, had to be rebuilt before the season started.

Swanberg: In 2001 and 2002, we started rebuilding South Lake Shore Drive south to the Animal Bridge at Marquette Road. The big emphasis was in concert with the Lakefront Restoration Program because the lake was at a record high level and because the breakwater had started to collapse the South Drive near 59th Street and there was flooding every time we had a major storm. The storm drainage to take the water away didn't exist and the topography was such that the water would just lay in the Drive and they would have to shut it down a couple of times a year. There is a stretch there where the Drive gets really close to the lake.

Monroe Street looking north across
Millennium Park towards Lakeshore East,
c. 2009. (Courtesy of The Walsh Group).

So, besides just a general upgrade, we had half a dozen contracts to rebuild the South Drive, and probably a dozen more to do breakwater restoration on the lake. Those two projects together were designed to keep the water out of the park and the roads. So the job was repaving, making the park and the roadway more friendly and making sure that the water that did get on to the Drive could safely get back into the lake. And, that part of the city had combined sewer, which means that we had sanitary and storm sewer running through one pipe. Chicago still does have that problem, and what happens today is that in normal flow, all the water, storm and sanitary goes to the treatment plant. But, in high flow, they go over diversions and all the storm and raw sewage goes into the lake. All the Lake Shore Drive South jobs changed that program to dedicated sanitary and dedicated storm. So, now all the storm flows into the lake and the sanitary cannot divert into the lake and goes where it is supposed to go into the treatment plants.

Walsh: We were involved in the Deep Tunnel which started back in the 1970s and is still going on today. Deep Tunnel absolutely met the goal that the city wanted, because without it the storm water was going into people's basements and now the water goes into the Deep Tunnel and eventually gets siphoned off into the treatment plants. The water gets treated there and then released into the river. Although in bad storms the excess is put into the lake, I would guess tthat happens rarely in comparison to what it would have been prior to the Deep Tunnel.

Swanberg: One of the projects that we did when we rebuilt South Lake Shore Drive was that we put in a series of pedestrian underpasses right outside the Museum of Science and Industry while they were building the underground parking garage in front. They had some construction issues and we helped them out with some of the technology we had for doing earth retention with small amounts of vibration and dewatering to facilitate their garage. We did excavate all of the material out in front of the Museum of Science and Industry for pedestrian access. As for other work on Grant Park besides constructing Millennium Park, we rebuilt the Balbo Drive Bridge, we rebuilt the Roosevelt Avenue Bridge, we rebuilt the Congress Street Bridge, and we rebuilt Montgomery Ward Park on the west side of the railroad tracks from Roosevelt to Congress. We did historic renovation of all those park elements. Near Lincoln Park, we did an historic renovation of the Academy of Sciences building which is now the headquarters for Lincoln Park Zoo. (Walsh: Dale was the project manager on that.)

Aerial view of South Lake Shore Drive looking towards downtown, c. 2009. (Courtesy of The Walsh Group).

Aerial view of Navy Pier, Chicago Harbor and Lake Shore Drive, co. 2009. (Courtesy of The Walsh Group).

Illinois Central Railroad tracks and Michigan Avenue skyscrapers, c. 2009. (Courtesy of The Walsh Group).

Swanberg: We have done half a dozen projects with Lincoln Park Zoo, including redoing the Silverback Gorilla Habitat, the Swan Pond (Walsh: That was my favorite.), part of the Lion exhibit and the Gateway Pavilion on the east side entrance of the Park.

Walsh: We did some of the seawalls going north on Lake Shore Drive, but we didn't do any of the paving work on North Lake Shore Drive.

Swanberg: But, we rebuilt Belmont Harbor and Diversey Harbor.

Walsh: We look at our work as contracts and not as history. We are making a living doing this and you guys are trying to recreate the history of the Drive. We built Jackson Park Harbor, Burnham Harbor, along with Belmont Harbor and Diversey Harbor and the seawall all the way around on the lake side and harbor side. I can tell you about something that is going to happen at the Oak Street "S" curve and the beach. That is going to be straightened out and those plans are on the drawing board and we have actually done some preliminary pricing for that project. Sometime in the next ten years—if they ever get the money—it will be done. The Outer Drive will go straight from the curve all the way to North Avenue and the beach will be extended out or a couple thousand yards into the lake.

Swanberg: We were involved in doing all of the infrastructure work for City Front Center, including the Ogden Slip and North Pier, and we built DuSable Harbor. And, some of the work that we did on South Lake Shore Drive involved the ponds that Olmsted designed behind the Museum of Science and Industry.

Walsh: I think that the world class view from the Drive, as far as I am concerned, is from the Promontory in front of the Adler Planetarium looking back on the city. And on southbound Lake Shore Drive, if you started at Monroe going south on the Drive, that always is a breathtaking view for me. When we started the job of rebuilding Grant Park at the south end near the Field Museum some 15 years ago, we started digging up the old cinders and remnants of the Great Chicago Fire. We found bottles and other remains of the Fire that still smelled of the fire. You have to remember that the ashes and trash from the Chicago Fire were pushed into the lakefront and that became Grant Park.

Ice Skating rink at Millennium Park, c. 2009.
(Courtesy of The Walsh Group).

Swanberg: We would stop work between five and six p.m. and the Field Museum staff would come over at night and walk through our spoil piles pulling out treasures, including liquor bottles, beer bottles, all sorts of trinkets and clothing. This was in 1996.

Walsh: We were fascinated with this buried memorabilia and the fact that nobody was very interested in it. There was so much of it that was just garbage from the Fire. Anybody can dig it up today. However, one amateur archeologist was found dead in one of our excavations. He was out there poking around over a weekend, just picking up bottles and trash, and died there.

Swanberg: There was an old elevator shaft where one of the terminus of the freight tunnel came right up at about Roosevelt and Columbus. There was about an 80' deep shaft that went down to the freight tunnel and we had to go down there and uncover it because it all had been buried. The shaft was used to move coal from the underground freight car and dump it on the lakefront. The area was all trash.

Lakefront skyscrapers, Monroe Harbor
and Lake Shore Drive, 2010.
(Courtesy, Eric Bronsky Collection).

Walsh: When Samuel Insull built the coal tunnel system, one of the terminus points was Roosevelt Road right near the I.C. Station.

Swanberg: So, they had an elevator in the shaft, and the coal cars would dump their ashes there. The elevator came up the shaft, and the ashes were dumped into the lake. It was my understanding that there was a series of wood trestles that went along the lakefront. So, the ash came up this elevator shaft and the dump cars would ride the trestle and dump it straight down. When the ash built up to the bottom of the trestle, they would just move the trestle out another 30'-50' and they would just keep filling and walking their way out. When we went down in the freight tunnel we found an old locomotive down there.

Walsh: These are little, low-profile mining locomotives used as diggers. They are small scale so they could fit into those tunnels. The folks who worked the tunnel in Insull's day just left the locomotive there.

Swanberg: So, we contacted the Illinois Railway Museum and gave it to them.

Walsh: As for buildings along Lake Shore Drive and nearby, we have done the Blue Cross-Blue Shield Building right on the park, the Shoreham, and the Tides in Lakeside East. On Michigan Avenue, we have done the Heritage, the Legacy, and the Columbian at Roosevelt Road. Right now, we are doing 2520 N. Lakeview which is on the inside of the lagoon and the harbor. It is the old Columbus Hospital. Actually, we are preserving Mother Seton's bones in a chapel that is right in the middle of the site. When the land was purchased, the nuns who owned it and sold it required in the deed that the little chapel with the bones be preserved. So we are building this giant, $250 million project around that chapel.

We did the major work on North Pier Terminal and Ogden Slip area for Charles Gardner, which was the original infrastructure when the Chicago Dock and Canal Trust finally decided to lease out (not sell) their land for 100 years to places like the Sheraton Hotel. My recollection is that Abraham Lincoln's signature is on the original Chicago Dock and Canal trust documents. He was the lawyer for the Illinois Central Railroad at that time and did all the legal work for the North Pier Terminal at Ogden Slip.

RICHARD WARD | I am a Mechanical Engineer who attended the Illinois Institute of Technology (IIT) and graduated in 1959. I was a U.S. Navy pilot and then I became a United Airlines pilot. I was on the city council in Des Plaines for about 15 years. Then I moved out to Island Lake, Illinois located out between Wauconda and Crystal Lake, and I became the chairman of the planning commission in Island Lake for a number of years. I moved down to the New East Side here to Harbor Point in 1998. So, I've been down here for about twelve years now. Because of my municipal background in planning (I was chairman of the Finance Committee in Des Plaines for about 12 of those 15 years), I looked around at what was going on in our area, in my new home, and realized there wasn't anybody really paying attention to what was going on in the area. The community did have an organization, called NEAR, which I joined in 1998 and am now president since 2006.

I began to study the development and accumulate all of the records from the plan development that started in 1969, and I ended up with several notebooks of all of the records (probably 95% of the records that exist). I realized that the developer was getting away with not meeting agreements that he had made with the city and each successive developer inherited the responsibility to complete those agreements. And, they weren't doing it.

This Illinois Central area, now being completed by Lakeshore East, has been called New East Side since 1991, and had originally been railroad tracks. In 1993, it became a golf course and, in 2001, a group led by Joel Carlins and Jim Loewenberg, who headed up the Magellan Corporation, became the lead developers.

Millennium Park sculptures,
Pritzker Pavilion, and The Heritage, 2010.
(Courtesy of The Walsh Group).

CHAPTER 6
PLANNING FOR THE FUTURE OF THE DRIVE AND THE "FINAL FOUR MILES" 2005–2010

PHIL ENQUIST | I run the urban planning group at Skidmore, Owings and Merrill and we are involved in a lot of cities, including new cities in China and also adjustments of existing cities, mostly in more urban areas. We try to stay focused on land that has already been built rather than going after green fields. We are always interested in trying to find a way to meet the demands of access without having roads dominate communities. We are always butting heads with traffic engineers that overdesign roads for peak capacity. A great example of that is the land in Glenview, Illinois at the Glen. People seem so worried about moving cars that they forget what you are really trying to do is move people who are biking and walking and in cars, so streets have to be public for all modes of transportation.

What is so great about Lake Shore Drive to me is that it is an event every time you drive it. You have this great relationship to the lake, to everyone out on the beaches, to people running on the paths or biking. You see all that activity and you feel like you are a part of it even though you are driving, and you enjoy the neighborhoods that you are passing. And it does seem to have a change in character as you go from one to the next. The great landscape medians by the Edgewater Beach area are beautiful, and every year they get better, and then in Lincoln Park you drive past the Diversey Harbor and the Lincoln Park lagoon where people are rowing. Then you get through downtown, and on your way to Hyde Park it changes again.

I always assumed that Lake Shore Drive was built in segments but I don't know the details of it. There is still the Inner Drive, and there is Lincoln Park West next to Lincoln Park, and there is East Lake Shore Drive by the Drake hotel.

There are a lot of roadways around the world that historically have access to waterfront communities and that have been done well. For examples, in Cannes, France, that waterfront road is very distinctive because all the hotels and residential buildings face that in a very civic way, and the beaches are on the other side. But, it is not carrying anywhere near the volume of traffic as Lake Shore Drive. So, in some ways, I think that Cannes has a better scale waterfront load. You have Pacific Coast Highway in California that runs through Del Mar and Solana Beach and other wonderful coastal communities. It does slow down so that you can cross it in places. But, it doesn't have our urban character. What Lake Shore

Aerial view of Lake Shore Drive, looking west
from the Gold Coast to Streeterville, 2010.
(Courtesy of Lawrence Okrent, Okrent Associates)

Drive has is very differen
somehow reflecting the
it's very urban. It is car
friendly, although it co
like a freeway and I th
will be on Lake Shore
where it is easier to
It's like the city
lake has an addres
if you drive throu
down the Near S
those areas. And
have that kind
similar to goin
conditions for
Shore Drive i
street to do j
I think that

Area Plan was one. For five years with the city, and then with Dan McCaffery, we have been doing the planning of South Works. Dan has been adamant that no one calls that Highway 41, but rather that we call it Lake Shore Drive and that Lake Shore Drive continues south. He very much wants that address for the whole South Works project.

I think that Lake Shore Drive is also a unifying factor for the city. Somehow, it isn't a main street, but it is the addressing street for Chicago. It does unify the city and there isn't any other street like it. You make a deliberate choice to take Lake Shore Drive, and where else can you drive for 19 miles and not see anything that is unattractive. When you drive south it is so dramatic to look at the downtown skyline from Lincoln Park and you are just aimed right at the John Hancock Building. My favorite entrance to Chicago is the Michigan Avenue off ramp from Lake Shore Drive because it is the joining of two really great streets. Also, I don't know a city that is more proactive than Chicago in the United States and where the community is so involved in making it a great city. I think that everybody understands that the stronger the city is, the better everyone's future is going to be. Look at almost every other Midwest and Great Lakes city and they are all struggling and losing jobs and they are cities where there isn't the same civic commitment as in Chicago.

ABNER MIKVA | When I was in the legislature, I got myself in all kinds of trouble with U.S. Steel that had one of the oldest steel mills in the country at 87th Street and the lake. They were employing 15,000 well-paid, steelworkers. They had this old plant that had been built in 1890 in which they were still closing off the blast furnace by three men ramming a pole into it. There was molten metal and slag all over the place. They were also dumping a lot of stuff into the lake. Their answer to the problem was to build a new plant in the lake, and I represented that area in the state legislature. Even though I was never one of Mayor Daley's "fair-haired boys" down there, and because it was my district, I had a lot of influence on the answer to the problem, and I made it clear that I was opposed to the idea of building a new plant in the lake. It was a good issue for me in Hyde Park and South Shore politically, but they sure did not like my view on the city's east side or in the 10th ward. The big parade in the 10th ward is Labor Day. I knew all these people and had been a steelworker union lawyer for years before I went into the state legislature. But, when I marched down the street with my wife and waving in the Labor Day parade, they yelled at me, "Hey, Commie, go back to Hyde Park! Take your lake with you." Because it's sort of like the way the Indianans felt about the Dunes. To them it's a job and it wasn't just a playground. The mill wasn't built.

One of the things that bothered me about this idea of putting a new steel mill out in the lake was that they were talking then about extending the Drive. It would have been a good idea, but not at the expense of using up so much lake. To this day, I still think I was right in opposing it, but none of those 15,000 jobs are left.

Every time I drive by there, or see it from the Skyway, I wonder whether we solved an environmental problem at the cost of 15,000 livelihoods—and that is expensive.

I worry about that issue, but, on the other hand, there is only one lake. The steel mills were an important piece of the economy of the East Side and the 10th Ward and the whole city. It was such a marvelous entry job for people who came over here from other countries or those who came north from the south. You didn't have to know much to work in the steel mills, you didn't need a college education, the wages were good, and the working conditions were good. A lot of steel workers put their children through college based on what they got at U.S. Steel.

I am an environmentalist because Enrico Fermi, the great nuclear scientist lived in Hyde Park and his widow, Laura Fermi, stayed there after he died and she was a strong supporter of mine. One time, at a political meeting when I was still in the state legislature, Laura was wearing this political button that said "Clean Air." I thought what a ridiculous button since whether air is clean or not clean has nothing to do with what we do. I made some comment and she started the education of Abner Mikva about the environment and I couldn't have had a better teacher. She made me aware how many of these things that we do have such an impact on the environment, and how many things we do that we don't know what the impact will have on the environment, such as when the U.S. Steel plant was originally built in Gary, Indiana. What better place to dump all that slag and other junk into Lake Michigan. It's right there and a big lake, and all that stuff would disappear. We have spent billions of dollars since then trying to clean it up and still haven't brought back all of the lake species that had been there. I still remember when we finally dedicated the Paul H. Douglas Lakeshore during the Nixon Administration and there was a Secretary of the Interior who was a good environmentalist. He spoke at the ceremony and talked about the lake. He said, "We ought to have learned that if we don't know the

Aerial view looking south from Belmont Harbor and Lakeview along Lake Shore Drive south towards downtown. 2010. (Courtesy of Lawrence Okrent, Okrent Associates).

consequences of our action on some of the important natural things, we should not do it." Those are irreplaceable assets we are given and we shouldn't despoil them.

DAN MCCAFFERY | When we make presentations about our former US Steel site, I don't allow anyone to call it Route 41 anymore. It is Lake Shore Drive. When you drive down there, Lake Shore Drive is just "God given." I must tell you that both God and Mayor Daley gave it, because from McCormick Place south it was once just a road. Today, it is the prettiest half of Lake Shore Drive by a multiple. It is gorgeous! In some respects, it is less urban because the right side and the left side of the Drive are somewhat "park-like" and, then, you are hit with the Museum of Science and Industry and it is so striking, and I think that it is unbelievable.

I tell people that if they think our South project isn't going to work, they should take a ride down south Lake Shore Drive for a change. We have that one little difficult spot around the South Shore Cultural Center to 79th Street where the roadway narrows. We are trying to get it made into two pairs of roads, so that the road there now will be made into a one-way road. Another road nearby will be one-way going north. And we will call them both the Lake Shore Drive

Extensions. We are doing that because, God willing, there is going to be so much traffic that there won't be a choice but to have two roads.

As for our timeline on the project, we are told now that the construction of the Extension of Lake Shore Drive through the project will be completed by September, 2012. Some is already completed. It seems a little bit long of a period of time, but they said that they can't do it any faster. Now, they are back at work after taking seven or eight months off, which really annoyed me. We are trying to accelerate that a little bit, because when it finishes we are supposed to have the shopping center completed for the project. The day that Lake Shore Drive finishes and is all connected we are going to have the shopping center completed at 79th. There are projected to be 13,500 units in the project when it is finished. If we line up this land with Navy Pier you would see that we are further out into the lake than the Pier. It is all land filled with 100% slag from the old US Steel Works that was poured directly into the lake. It is 40+ feet deep and goes out 300 feet.

As for Lake Shore Drive being urban America's most beautiful roadway, I don't think that there is a prettier place. And going south is not quite as urban in its feel. The unique thing about our project is that it will be a massive development east of Lake Shore Drive. We will be building east some three or four blocks.

Aerial view of Lake Shore Drive, Monroe Harbor, Buckingham Fountain, and South Michigan Avenue, with Hilton Hotel and Towers on right. 2010. (Courtesy of Lawrence Okrent, Okrent Associates).

The only private development in any way similar going north on the Drive is at Hollywood on Sheridan Road, but there it is only a block west.

As for how many people will live at the site and when it will be completed, we don't think that it will be done any quicker than 20 years and, hopefully, no longer than 25-30 years. The project is a mix of housing with high rises, low rises, town homes, and everything imaginable. There are going to be 13,000 homes there and we would say that there could be 25,000-30,000 people living in the complex. You would almost replace the number of workers who were at the US Steel plant when it was fully operational. The land had been cleaned by US Steel, and we only had a couple pockets to clean on the site. We will have to dig up the site because there are absolutely no services here now, including water, sewers, and electricity.

My favorite downtown project was the Hotel Burnham on State and Washington. Others include Nike Town, above Saks Fifth Avenue, and The Bernardin, off of Michigan at Chicago and Wabash.

No, I didn't grow up here. I came to Chicago almost 26 years ago in 1984. I was born in Ireland and moved to Canada at age 12. My entire family is from Ireland.

Aerial view of South Lake Shore Drive, including Illinois Central Railroad tracks and Hyde Park. 2010. (Courtesy of Lawrence Okrent, Okrent Associates).

JOHN NORQUIST | Lake Shore Drive is congested right now because CDOT is trying to turn it into a freeway. Traditionally, urban thoroughfares, going back to the ancient Romans and Greeks, had three purposes: movement, economic purpose of the marketplace, and social. Well, in a park, it is just going to be two: movement and social. But, when you have a road that is totally devoted to vehicles, it clashes with the park. You can have drives in a park, but they must be narrow enough so that they really don't destroy the park, like the way it transverses in Central Park in New York City.

Right now the only places you can get across Lake Shore Drive to get to the lake if you are downtown is at Monroe, Jackson and Balbo. If they allowed parking on the downtown section of Lake Shore Drive then people could get to the beach more easily. In Grant Park, the street is curbed, guttered and flat, with sidewalks on each side. It looks like a street but it has been completely turned over to vehicles. Parking could easily be allowed again on the two outside lanes on that portion of Lake Shore Drive between Randolph and Monroe and then to the Field Museum, it's built like a street and it looks like a street and it is, in fact, a big boulevard. If you just put a row of parking on each side of the Drive, it would instantly look like an easier street to cross for pedestrians at the intersections.

The traffic would slow down a little bit and it wouldn't really affect congestion that much because people would just use other routes. If they wanted to go fast they would go on I-94. People would reorganize their trips.

In Lincoln Park, the North Avenue Bridge is kind of a failure because if you see one of these things with screens on it to protect cars, that is really an indicator the design failed as it looks pretty ugly. That is a sign that they made a mistake going north from downtown Chicago where the grades separated Lake Shore Drive completely. If there were a few at-grade stop signs along the way, the traffic would behave even better. If you look at the great boulevards like those in Nice, France or Ipanema Beach in Rio (Rio is a city that is even bigger in population than Chicago), they have a lot of traffic. But, a lot of the waterfront streets are urban and they don't have freeways basically blocking access to the waterfront and that is one of the reasons that Rio is such a successful city. If you have a great city you shouldn't make it a place that has as its primary purpose someplace to drive through. I wouldn't put in more tunnels because you will just make it more like a freeway, and the more you separate the pedestrians from Lake Shore Drive, the more it will turn into a freeway. And, if it turns into a freeway it will lose its effectiveness and no longer be a boulevard.

Lake Shore Drive is definitely a hybrid road, a parkway that is both a boulevard and a freeway. It is not a formal boulevard like Logan Boulevard or Archer with access roads at the side of the road, but it is a parkway in the sense that Olmsted and other late 19th and early 20th century designers like Burnham designed it. If you had complete grade separation from Hollywood to the Museum of Science and Industry, the road would lose its character. It would all become more like it is today at McCormick Place where I-55 comes directly in, which is the only connection to the Interstate system that is direct. The McCormick Place section is unarguably the ugliest portion of Lake Shore Drive. Ohio Street, which was originally meant to go all the way as a freeway to Lake Shore Drive, was stopped at Orleans. I think that it should be rolled back all the way to the Kennedy and so the ramps are just like they are to the south, like Jackson where the ramps are tucked up real close against the freeway. As soon as you come off the freeway, you come on to Jackson and quickly you are at the exact same scale of Jackson as it is as a street through downtown. Whereas, with the Ohio Street ramps, you may as well be in the middle of Ohio because you are driving at a really fast speed through the complexity of the city, and it is completely inappropriate.

Aerial view of Grant Park, Museum Campus, and downtown, looking north on Lake Shore Drive. 2010. (Courtesy of Lawrence Okrent, Okrent Associates).

Chicago's politics are complicated and real estate owners have power because of the "machine" nature of politics. The "Machine" is more likely to listen to somebody who is vested. In fact, the reason that the ramps are so tight up on the Kennedy in the downtown area is because the property owners didn't want their property taken and the Machine listened in a way that Illinois DOT would not. All of these things have influenced the hybrid nature of Lake Shore Drive.

When, you move north toward downtown, and as you get closer to I-55 the Drive becomes a freeway and the road is more important than the people, Chicago or Lake Michigan. The concrete structure is completely dominant and hideous. Then you get past McCormick Place, and, gradually, Soldier Field warns you that the road is going to change for the better, and there is a stoplight, and you are back in the wonderfully complex city of Chicago. IDOT and some of the people in the city government are in a constant fight between the engineers who want to speed up the traffic and the planners and some traffic engineers who are more reform-minded and who want to try to keep it a street. If IDOT had its way Lake Shore Drive would be a freeway, and all of Lake Shore Drive would look like it does at McCormick Place.

I think that the work of the Friends of the Parks has been very important in terms of landscaping and beautifying Lake Shore Drive. The coalition discourages those who want to try to turn the Drive into a freeway. The plantings don't affect the physical driving, but it is a signal that you are not on a freeway, but that you are on what amounts to a parkway. So, then we move north through some really elegant bridges with grade separations on them which are the earliest ones on Lake Shore Drive when you go through North Avenue and Fullerton and over the boat harbor. Where it comes through there is this beautiful art deco bridge and it is that way all the way up to Foster. That creates the hybrid that really works well and the grade separations are as well done as they can be. The ramps are narrow, there is queuing at Belmont which some people find is a problem.But, the fact that there is queuing at Belmont helps to make some of the traffic go somewhere else, and experienced drivers know that is coming. Then you get up to Foster, where the Drive used to end, and it really wasn't an improvement or really helped Lake Shore Drive to extend it to Hollywood. The problem is that wherever you ended the Drive you were going to have a street like Ridge Boulevard, and you still could have had the park without the roadway, and Ridge is one of the most unpleasant streets to walk on in Chicago.

As for extending the Drive past Hollywood and ending it further north, there are several bad things that would happen. The opposition to it is mostly the property owners and residents who live close to the lake, with the most fervent being the ones who live east of Sheridan Road who would lose these wonderful direct lake connections at Lunt, Morse, Farwell, Pratt, Columbia, Albion and North Shore. Those are all beach connections that are just fabulous and world class. So, if you brought Lake Shore Drive along there, it could be done elegantly and you could try to make it like it is between Fullerton and Foster. But, that would take a lot of care, and for people who live close that would be a horrible loss and they will fight it. Those of us who live further west of Sheridan also have concerns. If the Drive is extended, more traffic will be drawn to the Drive. People who might now tend to use the Edens may be attracted to the Drive.

I still have mixed feelings about calling Lake Shore Drive a roadway because it is in the city, and I feel that it is a hybrid. To me it is the most interesting one because it is very beautiful and there is a really, really strong juxtaposition of the city's urbanism, like the Gold Coast, Lake Shore Drive, Grant Park and the lake. For Chicago, Lake Shore Drive is the equivalent of New York's Central Park because of the juxtaposition of the urban scene and the lake, and Lake Shore Drive doesn't ruin that view because it is not a freeway. Chicago has such a strong, powerful building landscape in its downtown, Gold Coast and Lincoln Park. From a functional standpoint, Lake Shore Drive does carry a lot of the commuter load without being hideous except for the area around McCormick Place.

I think that Soldier Field and the museums saved Lake Shore Drive. If they weren't there, then that whole ugliness from I-55 would extend further, and having this ugly behemoth come busting into Lake Shore Drive is not a civilized act. So, what they could do is after the intersection of I-55 and I-94, it should taper down quickly and become a multi-lane boulevard, and then become an urban street as it connects with Lake Shore Drive. That would create tremendous real estate options in that corridor and the city would benefit from maybe $1 billion or $2 billion in investment if that were a magnificent street. And, then, Lake Shore Drive would benefit because there would be an opportunity to take that really ugly portion from Chinatown into the Drive and it would become better. You would have to tear that down and start all over again, but the freeway infrastructure lasts about 40 years before you have to completely rebuild it anyway. There will be opportunities to fix that portion of Lake Shore Drive and I-55, but maybe not in our lifetime. Right now that is the most degraded section so there is no way you could say that is America's most beautiful roadway there. You can say that south of there, you can say that north of there.

North Lake Shore Drive, across eight lanes of traffic. ca 2010 (Courtesy Eric Bronsky Collection).

MARSHALL SULOWAY | I was Commissioner of Public Works for the city in the 1970s. I recall that in the 1940s and 1950s, the Drive was extended, first to Bryn Mawr, then to Foster and finally to Hollywood. They got the land for the extension from Foster to Hollywood from construction sites like the Congress Street Expressway. I worked on that project and I was with the IDOT at that time. From Halsted Street going west about seven miles, it is mostly a "depressed" highway. We excavated between bridges and they wrecked the buildings on either side, excavated for the highway, and took the excavation digs up to Foster for use as the landfill for the extension of Lake Shore Drive. By doing the fill that way, the state and city were saving money because the excavators had a place to put the diggings and it was valuable to those who were extending the Drive.

From 1949 to 1964, I was with IDOT as a district engineer, and then I went to the city. They wanted to extend the drive from Foster to Hollywood to spread out the traffic because everyone was getting off at Foster and driving north on Sheridan Road. The Edgewater Beach Hotel was already having financial problems in the '50s and the hotel gave away riparian rights for the beach to the city to build the extension of the Drive. It would have happened to the hotel whether or not the city had decided to extend the Drive from Foster to Hollywood.

On the South Side, the Hyde Park people fought against the widening of the Drive during the 1950s. They wanted a park-like drive and they were against an expressway with all of these light poles and the so-called "New Jersey rails." The residents of the neighborhood were afraid that the city was going to raise the speed limit on the Drive, and they were concerned that it would lead to the city and state cutting down a lot of trees along the lakefront in Hyde Park. When the Drive was rebuilt, there were 12 feet lanes constructed because of the new design. Just the idea of a wide expanse of concrete and the light poles irritated the neighborhood residents.

View of Lake Shore Drive from
North Avenue Overpass, 2010.
(Courtesy of Eric Bronsky Collection).

following page
View of South Lake Shore Drive in
Hyde Park, looking North toward Loop, 2010.
(Courtesy of Eric Bronsky Collection).

View of traffic on Lake Shore Drive,
looking North, 2010.
(Courtesy of Eric Bronsky Collection).

JAN SCHAKOWSKY | As the U.S. Congressional Representative for the lake front from Evanston to Diversey, I know that there is nothing more explosive or controversial than talking about altering Lake Shore Drive and the current lakefront configuration. There has also been talk in the past at Loyola University about additional landfill, short-lived consideration of a marina being built at Evanston and Howard Avenue, discussions about creating more green space and bike paths along the lake, and even proposals to implement the vision of Daniel Burnham and build islands off the shore. Hundreds of people participate in community meetings, offer suggestions and opinions, and engage their elected officials. The tremendous passion is a reflection of how central the lake is to our community including the people who live right at the lake, those that enjoy the parks and beaches, and the many who simply appreciate driving along beside it.

It's is a wonderful thing that Chicagoans feel a sense of ownership and entitlement about our lakefront. No big city on the Great Lakes other than Chicago has dedicated almost the entire length to public land for everyone to enjoy. It's the reason that so many new visitors are surprised at just how beautiful Chicago is. They almost always mention taking a drive down Lake Shore Drive.

I don't know if there are changes on the horizon for our section of Lake Shore Drive. What I do know for sure is that nothing will happen without a process that fully involves the community in the decision-making. The City of Chicago, the Park District, Friends of the Park and all of the local officials know that all the stakeholders, especially the local residents, want to be and need to be at the table. Nothing is considered more sacred to North Side residents that our beloved lakefront.

ROBERT GORDON | I can remember personal experiences when I tried to cross Lake Shore Drive at the Buckingham Fountain on my bike and on foot. The crossing lights were very poorly timed and nobody respected them and they weren't very well marked. Eventually, the mayor closed down the crossing there which leaves almost half a mile between where you can actually cross Lake Shore Drive, and it is terrible. For a while, people were just running across the drive and jumping over the bollards.

Since I am an architect, I proposed a solution. I noticed that Queen's Landing and the level of the plateau there was well above Lake Shore Drive. So, without changing the level and keeping the landscape in the nature of Grant Park, you could just continue across Lake Shore Drive on a land bridge and walk down a simple ramp to the lake front with no interference to traffic, at all, and vice versa.

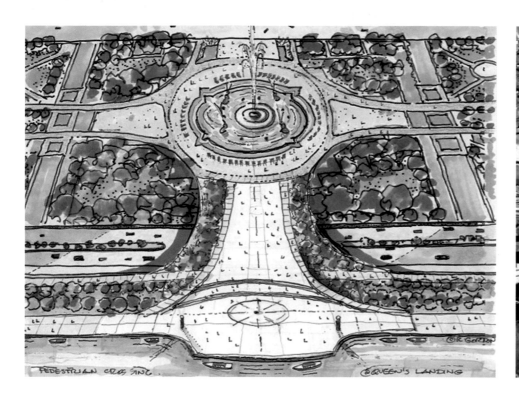

Queen's Landing Earth Bridge
(Courtesy of Robert Gordon Associates)

I thought it was a good idea and I presented it to Mayor Daley. In fact, at one point, the State Legislature had put aside about $29 million for Queen's Landing about 10 years ago. But, instead they ended up using the money for a new Metra station at Roosevelt Road, and that was a good thing to do as well.

However, it still leaves that problem. Buckingham Fountain was at one time the second largest site in Illinois for visitors, second only to Navy Pier. So, you have these millions of people during the summer who are looking at the lakefront, and they have to walk half a mile to get around to it. And, even then, they have to deal with traffic. So, for a while people were jumping the bollards by the fountain and I did a little video of different people and the traffic. Once I saw cars were all stopped and some pedestrians even jumped on the hoods of cars to get across. They were all screaming at each other and walking between the cars. I didn't think that was a good solution to the problem.

It might take a little bit of the lowering of Lake Shore Drive, as well, but the landing would be significantly above the lakefront and be safe for pedestrians. At this point, it has been tabled because of financial issues. The mayor says he likes it, and everybody says that they need to do something there, but nothing is happening in the economy.

After I presented the Queen's Bridge idea to the mayor, I was at a meeting of his landscape committee and a similar plan was offered but with a suspension bridge designed by Calatrava. The idea, and the mayor hated it, was to basically take the same bridge idea but to build two large pylons which would take away from Buckingham Fountain. So, we had a suspension bridge idea, and while Calatrava's design was beautiful it would have worked better somewhere else.

ERMA TRANTER | Friends of the Parks was formed in 1975 by Lois Weisberg, Vickie Ranney, Cindy Mitchell and others when the park system had been politicized and people got jobs because of their political involvement and not because they were qualified to work in parks. The result was that the parks were in shambles, so it was formed in '75. I came on board when I received my MA in Urban Planning and I started working here in 1981, and have been working ever since on lakefront parks, neighborhood parks and children's playgrounds.

We worked with Skidmore, Owings and Merrill many times over the years. Skidmore has a very long and deep history in the city of Chicago, and they have done some pro bono things for a lot of citizens' groups. We asked for their help on the "Last Four Miles" plan for the Drive which we have worked on since 2006. It is community based planning that focuses on the question of how the city would complete the park system that doesn't exist yet. Lake Shore Drive was part of the reason why we had a continuation of parks built north through the 1950s up to Hollywood because it was federal funding for the Drive, and then you could build parkland to the east at that location for recreation. But, it ended in the 1950s when the Drive was extended to Hollywood and there is no way to continue going up to Evanston if you are walking or running or taking your kid for a bicycle ride. So, there are two miles on the north end of the Drive that we consider to be unfinished. And, if you go south you could run all the way down to the South Shore Cultural Center at 71st Street and then you run out of parkland and that means that there are two miles on the South Side that have yet to be completed.

Our plan that we worked on with the community was different. On the North Side, the community did not want an extension of Lake Shore Drive. They actually opposed our plan because they thought it would be driven by Lake Shore Drive funding, and it isn't. On the South Side, I think our park plan which we are starting to implement right now, is definitely going to happen. The first piece of it is the old Iroquois Steel land. You have U.S. Steel at

around 79th Street, but then you had Iroquois Steel at around 90th Street. That land has been cleaned and the steel manufacturing left decades ago, and it was given to the Port Authority who is not using the land. So, we are hoping that the first part of the last "Four Miles" on the South Side would be to transfer that land from about 90th Street to 95th Street to the Park District.

Lake Shore Drive, which is basically a neighborhood street from 71st Street to 83rd, would change into a boulevard where they have a little more width at 79th Street where the U.S. Steel facility was located. Unfortunately, from 71st to 79th Streets, there is housing on either side. So, there aren't plans that I have seen to do anything other than curbs, gutters and resurfacing. But, there is little more of a designed landscape plan that is happening from 79th Street southward.

As for Oak Street Beach in the future, there is a planning grant available now. The CDOT oversees that location as the local governmental agency, and they have a grant to study how that curve could be straightened. There will be a lot of community involved in talking about that, and I think that it will be an opportunity to create more parkland to the east between Ohio and Oak Street. At this point, when you come in off Ohio Street there are two streets that end at Navy Pier

(Grand and Illinois). But, you get to Ohio Street and you have parkland there, and folks can bike underneath where Lake Point Tower is located, and you can bike between Ohio and Oak Street, but there is no real grass there and it is just a concrete slab that is about 50' wide. The planning for Oak Street (and there are many ideas being explored) includes the suggestion to straighten it and then add considerable lake fill into the lake on the east to create more green park space. That varies because some people have proposed 200 feet of width put in there, and I have seen a variety of ideas. If it is the case that they do have that grant to study it, then there will be major public involvement. But, it will be a good opportunity to kind of tweak a section of Lake Shore Drive that has some safety issues and isn't very attractive. You have magnificent buildings on the west side, the lake on the east, but that narrow piece of concrete there is unfortunate. This occurred because of the weak original design we had for that portion of the Drive.

Oak Street beach was originally just concrete and there wasn't a beach there. Then, using sand as a fill combined with Mother Nature's natural drift of sand from the north to the south of the lake, you have a big beach plus the water level of the lake is down so as the water level goes down you get more exposure to the beach.

Chicago was lucky enough to have had a group of remarkable visionaries some 140 years ago who said the lakefront belongs to everyone. I haven't seen that in other places. We were really blessed with visionaries such as Daniel Burnham, Jens Jensen, Alfred Caldwell, and Frederick Law Olmsted(who had a hand in the lakefront park system on the city's South Side). The lake was seen as a resource that in the future would do great things for the city of Chicago. So, we really are very blessed.

The second thing, though, was that the citizens of the city of Chicago were willing to pay for this beautification and preservation. They were willing to raise their property taxes in referenda because from 100 years ago, until the 1950s, we had binding referenda. The citizens had to approve of increasing their property taxes to get the work done. There were 72 referenda where they went to the citizens and asked them, "Will you increase your property taxes so that we can create Burnham Park from Roosevelt Road to 18th Street?" Then, they asked, "Will you approve the funding for 18th Street to 22nd Street?" And, the response from the citizens was, "Yes." All along, the citizens were willing to sacrifice additional funds so that that park system was public and beautiful.

Aerial view of northern end of Lake Shore
Drive at Hollywood Avenue and Sheridan Road,
2010. (Courtesy of Lawrence Okrent,
Okrent Associates).

And, since the 1950s, we have only done small things. The Park District hasn't done a lot of massive lake fill as they were doing with the earlier referenda, but they are doing small pieces. For example, the Park District has a plan to do a little lake fill at 47th Street to create a beach of 12-20 acres. Then, the Park District acquired the South Shore Cultural Center in the 1970s. At the time the community said and we said, this is public lakefront and the Park District had to buy that property, and they bought that. On the North Side, when the Claritian Fathers at Berger Park at 6200 North at the lakefront had a series of buildings across from Sacred Heart on the lakefront. They went up for private sale, but the community and the Friends of the Parks said that was lakefront and the Park District should acquire it, and they acquired it. When Walter Netsch saw that the Thunderbird Hotel between 75th and 76th Streets on the lake was up for sale, they bought that property, cleared it and created parkland.

So, the Park District is acquiring where they can the private pieces. I think that it is their responsibility to acquire whatever becomes available on the lakefront in those areas where we don't have parks. They have been doing it for 20-30 years. Our ultimate goal is to make it all parkland from border to border. We had Burnham and the folks who went before us with all those tax referenda they paid for by sacrificing their dollars to give us all that we have on the lakefront. It is our responsibility as well as the next generation to complete that task.

Aerial view of Lake Shore Drive,
including Lincoln Park and Diversey Harbor,
2010. (Courtesy of Lawrence Okrent,
Okrent Associates).

Rendering of Proposed Development at former U.S. Steelworks and extension of South Lake Shore Drive, 2010. (Courtesy of McCaffery Interests).

WASHINGTON PARK

THE UNIVERSITY OF CHICAGO

JACKSON PARK

SOUTH LAKESHORE DRIVE